Contents at a Glance

Table of Contents

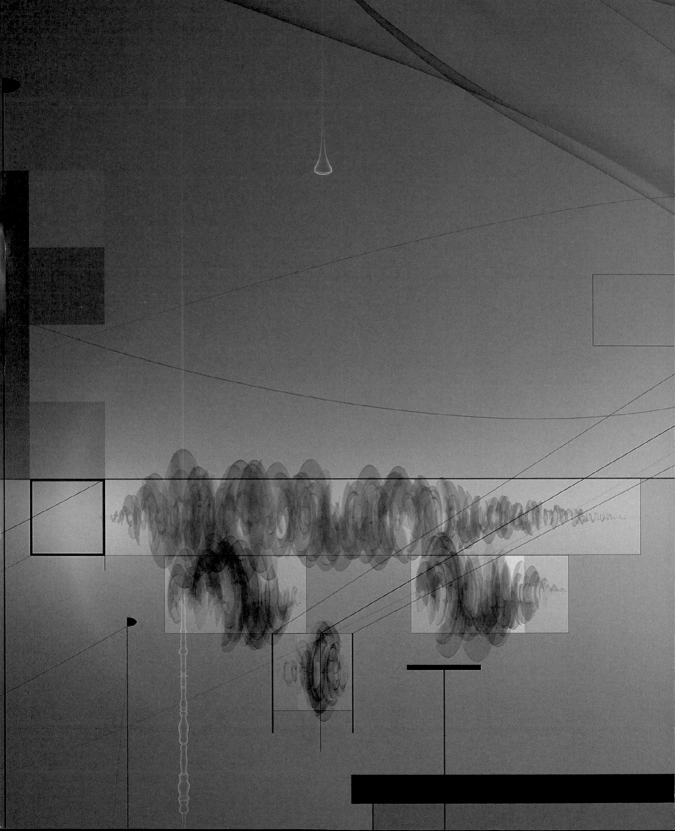

Getting Started

There's an old cliché in the motion picture world: Video is two-thirds audio. And it's true. Audiences don't mind a video that has the occasional dodgy edit or improperly balanced color. In fact, the eye is such an imprecise instrument of perception that people even enjoy watching badly compressed moving images on the web, stuttered and distorted as the video may be. But if your audio is even slightly less than perfect, viewers will switch channels or click to another website. "Noisy" audio is the bane of any video production; wildly fluctuating dialogue levels annoy viewers, and poorly mixed soundtracks seem to cause unbearable weight on the audience's ears. Using Soundtrack Pro, you can resolve all of these issues.

The book you are reading will introduce you to many audio problems that are common to video projects, and you'll learn some important solutions that will enhance the quality of your productions. As you read, keep in mind that this is an introductory-level book aimed at readers with no experience using Soundtrack Pro 2. Additionally, this book does not cover every problem that you might encounter while adjusting the audio for your productions. Instead, these lessons are designed as a springboard for further explorations into sound design with Soundtrack Pro 2.

If you read carefully through the steps, you will gain the knowledge you need to explore the deeper features of Soundtrack Pro 2 and adapt the program to fix any audio issues you may be experiencing. Learning how to edit audio is exactly the same as learning how to edit video: It takes time and practice. Welcome to the official Apple Pro Training Series course for Soundtrack Pro 2.

System Requirements

Before beginning to use *Apple Pro Training Series: Soundtrack Pro 2*, you should have a working knowledge of your computer and its operating system. Make sure that you know how to use the mouse and standard menus and commands and also how to open, save, and close files. If you need to review these techniques, see the printed or online documentation included with your system.

▶ A Macintosh computer with a 1.25 GHz or faster PowerPC G4, PowerPC G5, Intel Core Duo, or Intel Xeon processor

▶ 1 GB of RAM

▶ An AGP or PCI Express Quartz Extreme graphics card (Final Cut Studio is not compatible with integrated Intel graphics processors)

▶ A display with 1024 x 768 resolution or higher

▶ Mac OS X v10.4.9 or later

▶ QuickTime 7.1.6 or later

▶ A DVD drive for installation

▶ For 5.1 surround monitoring of multichannel audio content: an audio interface with a minimum of six outputs

▶ For multitrack recording: an audio interface with multiple inputs

Copying the Lesson Files

This book includes an *APTS Soundtrack Pro 2* DVD of all the necessary files you will need to complete the lessons. On the disc, you will find a disc image called **APTS-SoundtrackPro.dmg**. Open the lesson files from inside the disc image to avoid linking conflicts. If you drag the files out of the disc image,

Soundtrack Pro may not link to the correct media and you will need to relink your files (see "Reconnecting Broken Media Links" below).

The steps below show you how to open the **APTS-SoundtrackPro.dmg** disc image.

Installing the Lesson Files

1   Put the *APTS Soundtrack Pro 2* DVD into your computer's DVD drive.

2   Drag the **APTS-SoundtrackPro.dmg** disc image from the DVD to the desktop or a location on the hard disk.

3   Once the disc image has fully copied to your hard disk, double-click to mount it on your desktop. Look inside this mounted disc image to locate the individual lesson files.

4   To begin each lesson, open Soundtrack Pro, then follow the instructions at the beginning of the lesson to open the project files for that lesson.

Reconnecting Broken Media Links

In the process of copying the media from this book's DVD, you may break a link between the project file and the media file. If this happens, the next time you open a project file, a window will appear saying that Soundtrack Pro can't find a file and asking you to reconnect the project files. Reconnecting the project files is a simple process. Just follow these steps:

1   In the Can't Find File window, click the Find File button.

2   Navigate to where the Soundtrack Pro book files folder resides on your hard disk, then go to the specific Media subfolder.

3   Using the File Browser, in the appropriate Media subfolder, select the media file you wish to reconnect.

4   Click to select the Use Selected Path to Reconnect Other Missing Files checkbox.

5   Click the Choose button to reconnect all the media for that project.

6   Repeat steps 2 through 5 until all project files have been reconnected.

About the Apple Pro Training Series

Apple Pro Training Series: Soundtrack Pro 2 is part of the official training series for Apple Pro applications, developed by experts in the field and certified by Apple, Inc. The series offers complete training in all Apple Pro products. The lessons are designed to let you learn at your own pace. Although each lesson provides step-by-step instructions for creating specific projects, there's room for exploration and experimentation. You can progress through the book from beginning to end, or dive right into the lessons that interest you most. Each lesson concludes with a review section summarizing what you've covered.

Apple Pro Certification Program

The Apple Pro Training and Certification Program is designed to keep you at the forefront of Apple's digital media technology while giving you a competitive edge in today's ever-changing job market. Whether you're an editor, graphic designer, sound designer, special effects artist, or teacher, these training tools are meant to help you expand your skills.

Upon completing the course material in this book, you can become a certified Apple Pro by taking the certification exam at an Apple Authorized Training Center. Certification is offered in Final Cut Pro, DVD Studio Pro, Shake, Motion, Logic, Aperture, and Soundtrack Pro. Successful certification as an Apple Pro gives you official recognition of your knowledge of Apple's professional applications while allowing you to market yourself to employers and clients as a skilled, pro-level user of Apple products.

For those who prefer to learn in an instructor-led setting, Apple also offers training courses at Apple Authorized Training Centers worldwide. These courses, which use the Apple Pro Training Series books as their curriculum, are taught by Apple Certified Trainers and balance concepts and lectures with hands-on labs and exercises. Apple Authorized Training Centers have been carefully selected and have met Apple's highest standards in all areas, including facilities, instructors, course delivery, and infrastructure. The goal of the program is to offer Apple customers, from beginners to the most seasoned professionals, the highest-quality training experience. To find an Authorized Training Center near you, go to www.apple.com/software/pro/training.

Resources

Apple Pro Training Series: Soundtrack Pro 2 is not intended to be a comprehensive reference manual, nor does it replace the documentation that comes with the application. For more information about program features discussed in this book, refer to these resources:

► The Reference Guide. Accessed through the Soundtrack Pro Help menu, the Reference Guide contains a complete description of all features.

► Apple's website: www.apple.com.

1

Lesson Files APTS-SoundtrackPro > Lesson 01 > 01 Begin.fcp

Time This lesson takes approximately 30 minutes to complete.

Goals Open sequences from Final Cut Pro in Soundtrack Pro

Explore the Soundtrack Pro workspace

Set a sampling rate

Adjust the starting timecode

Explore playback techniques, including the use of J-K-L keys

Work with volume and pan settings

Learn about mute and solo functions

Export a song

Complete the roundtripping process back to Final Cut Pro

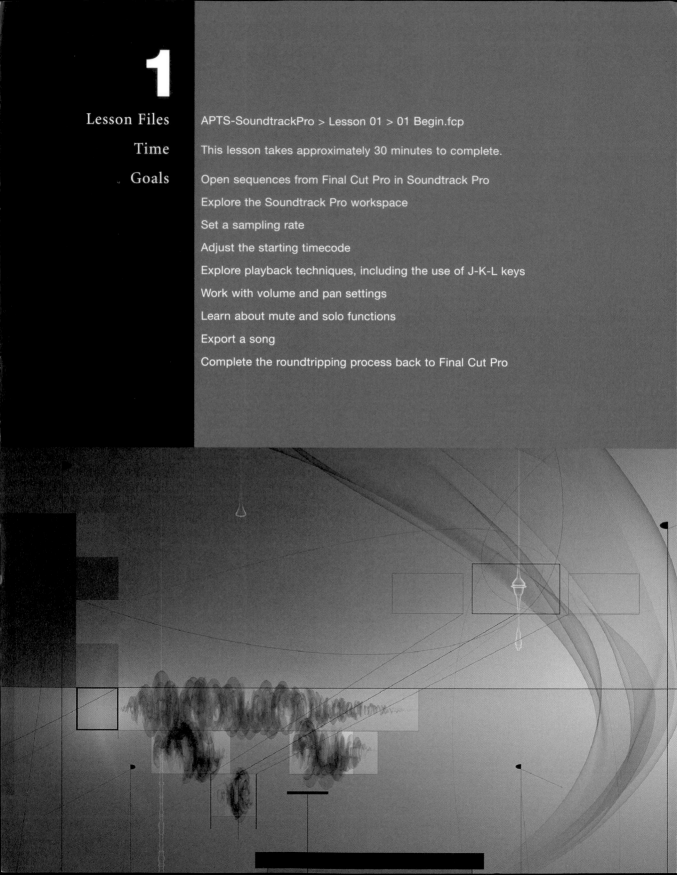

Roundtripping with Final Cut Pro

Final Cut Studio 2 gives you a full suite of video tools that have been designed from the ground up to work together to create professional-quality video productions. Final Cut Pro 6 is the nonlinear editing tool at the heart of the bundle, and Soundtrack Pro 2 is the audio postproduction tool that accompanies it. With this new version of Soundtrack Pro, you'll find enhanced tools for integrating the workflow between the two applications, and a big part of that workflow is "roundtripping," or the process of opening a sequence (or project file) from Final Cut Pro, editing the sequence in a helper application like Soundtrack Pro, and then returning the finished files to Final Cut Pro for further editing.

In this lesson you'll explore the roundtrip process. Along the way you'll take an introductory look at the Soundtrack Pro workspace and learn some important techniques for customizing the interface, playing audio clips, and navigating around your projects. At the end of the lesson, you'll discover the streamlined process for returning your finished audio files to Final Cut Pro. There's a lot to learn, so let's jump right in.

Opening Sequences from Final Cut Pro

To begin the process of roundtripping, let's open a project in Final Cut Pro, take a quick look around, and then send the project to Soundtrack Pro.

> **NOTE ▶** At the end of this lesson, you'll send the output file from Soundtrack Pro back to your Final Cut Pro Timeline and complete the roundtrip process.

1 Open the file **01 Begin.fcp** in the Lesson 01 folder.

A sequence opens in Final Cut Pro.

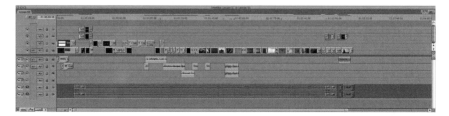

2 Play the sequence and watch the action to get a good feel for the sounds in this project and what sounds might need to be added.

Sending Sequences to Soundtrack Pro

Now that you know the media you're working with, it's time to send the Final Cut Pro sequence to Soundtrack Pro.

1   In Final Cut Pro's Browser, select the sequence titled *01-Begin*.

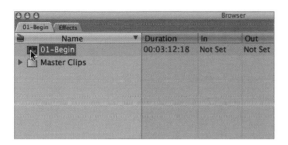

NOTE ▶ Selecting the sequence in the Browser ensures that the entire sequence and all the audio clips it contains are sent to Soundtrack Pro. As you'll see in later lessons, you can also send individual clips to Soundtrack Pro for editing, but more on that later.

2   Choose File > Send To > Soundtrack Pro Multitrack Project.

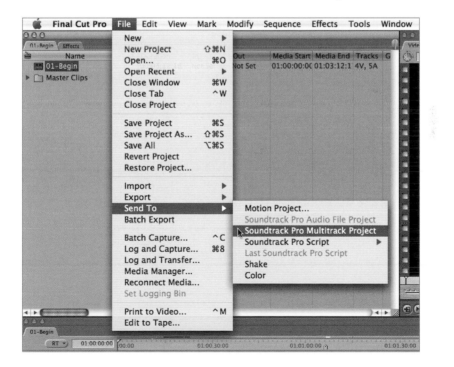

A Save dialog appears.

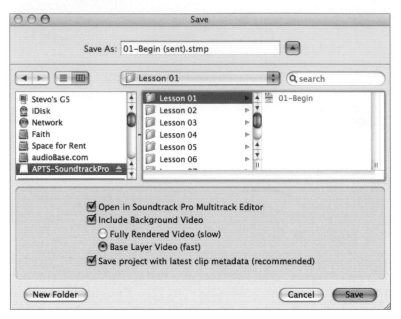

This dialog is used to save a Soundtrack Pro project file that you will edit. There are a lot of settings at the bottom of this Save dialog. You'll explore these in detail in later lessons. For now, let's save the sequence as a new Soundtrack Pro project with the current settings selected.

3   Navigate to a folder on your hard disk where you want to save the new Soundtrack Pro project.

4   Click the Save button.

Final Cut Pro renders the audio and video into a format that Soundtrack Pro can read, and then opens the project in Soundtrack Pro.

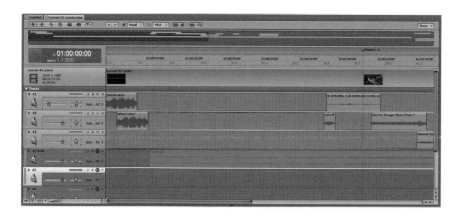

Soundtrack Pro Overview

Right now you're looking at Soundtrack Pro's main editing workspace, called the Multitrack Editor. Indeed, if you look at the top-center portion of this workspace, you'll see several rows containing clips. Each of these rows is called a track, and these tracks are used to organize audio clips to make a soundtrack. Of course, there's a lot of other stuff going on here, so let's take a quick look around.

Working with Panes

Somewhat like the interface in other Apple applications, such as DVD Studio Pro or Motion, both of which have a main window organized into multiple panes, Soundtrack Pro's single-window workspace is divided into panes, and each pane holds tabs that contain editing functions. If you are using a large display, you may find it easiest to work with all of Soundtrack Pro's panes displayed at once. However, if screen real estate is tight, it may be more convenient to display only the pane(s) you are currently working in so you can see more of the Multitrack Editor. Let's look at hiding and displaying panes now.

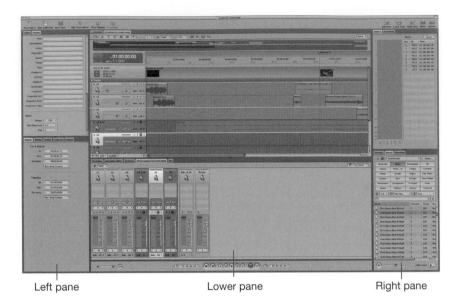

Left pane   Lower pane   Right pane

1   In the upper-right corner of the workspace, click the Right Pane button in
     the Toolbar.

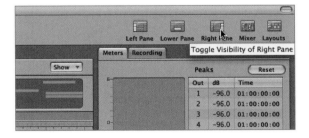

The right pane is hidden, and the Multitrack Editor becomes wider. This
gives you more horizontal space to edit your tracks. If you're editing a long
soundtrack, then more horizontal space means you can see more of your
project in detail, at a glance. As you work with Soundtrack Pro, you'll find
yourself hiding and showing panes all the time as you balance the need to
see your project in detail in the Multitrack Editor against the need to use
the functions contained in the tabs located in the various panes.

NOTE ▶ You can't hide the middle pane that contains your tracks. Additionally, depending on the resolution of the monitor you are using, some parts of the GUI won't be visible with all the panes open (such as the timecode value sliders in the transport controls).

Let's toggle the visibility of the right pane to display it once again, using a slightly different technique.

2   Choose Window > Toggle Right Pane (Control-D).

The right pane reappears.

NOTE ▶ The keyboard shortcuts for displaying the left, bottom, and right panes are adjacent to one another on the keyboard, with the left key (A) toggling the left pane, the right key (D) toggling the right pane, and the center key (S) toggling the lower pane.

Working with Tabs

Each tab in the workspace contains a group of similar editing functions. You can rearrange these tabs at will, moving them from pane to pane or even dragging them out of their host pane to open a new window. Soundtrack Pro's interface is all about choice and customization—using tabs, you can set up the workspace any way you like.

1   In the bottom portion of the left pane, drag the Effects tab out of the pane, and then release the mouse button.

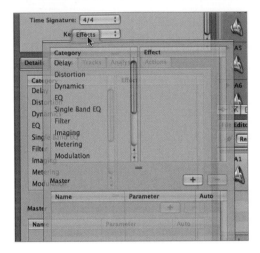

A floating pane is created, holding only the Effects tab.

NOTE ▶ If you have multiple displays attached to your computer, keep this trick in mind, as it's the best way to spread Soundtrack Pro's workspace across your displays.

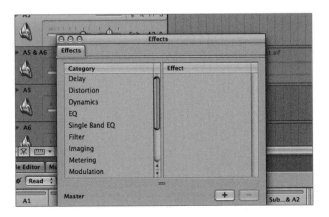

You can also move tabs to other panes, which allows you to customize the workspace to your individual workflow requirements. This is particularly important if you find you often need to see certain tabs at the same time while editing.

2   Drag the Effects tab until it's directly beside the Recording tab in the right pane.

> **NOTE ▶** A blue box will appear around the tabs to indicate when you are in the correct location to drop the tab.

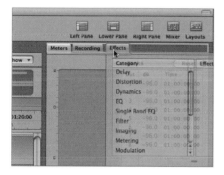

The Effects tab is added to the right pane, beside the Recording tab. You can also move tabs around inside their panes to reorganize the way they are displayed.

3   Drag the Effects tab to the left of the Meters tab.

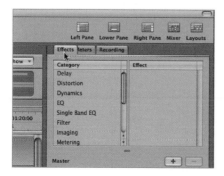

As you drag the tab, the Recording and Meters tabs jump out of the way.

Using Window Layouts

Window layouts are preset window arrangements that you can jump between while editing in Soundtrack Pro. Out of the box, you get two window layouts, the default standard layout and a "Separate Mixer and Video" layout that is particularly suited to users with two active displays. You can also create and save your own custom window layouts to tailor the workspace to your particular editing requirements.

The following steps show you how window layouts work. You'll start by creating a custom layout to save the changes you've made to the workspace, before resetting the workspace to the default layout.

1   To save your customized window layout, choose Window > Save Layout.

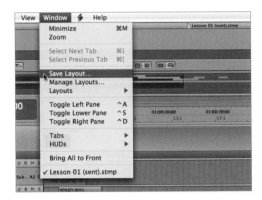

A Save dialog drops down from Soundtrack Pro's title bar.

2   Type *My Window Layout*, and click the Save button.

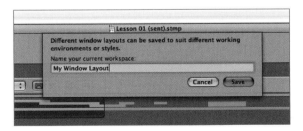

The window layout is saved.

3   Choose Window > Layouts.

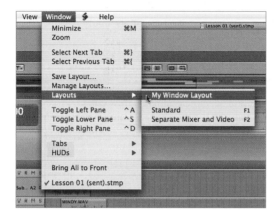

Notice that your new custom window layout is at the top of the list of window layouts that appears. Below it are listed the two window layouts that come with Soundtrack Pro.

NOTE ▶ To delete a window layout, go to the Window menu and choose the Manage Layouts option. Here you can rename or delete your custom window layouts.

4   Choose Window > Layouts > Standard (F1).

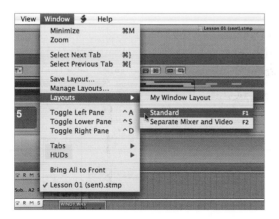

Soundtrack Pro returns to the default window layout.

Setting Project Properties

When you send a file from Final Cut Pro to Soundtrack Pro, the conversion process sets up your Soundtrack Pro project so that it closely matches the settings from your Final Cut Pro sequence. For example, the timecode will be either non-drop or drop frame, depending on the setting used in the source Final Cut Pro sequence. Similarly, the sampling rate will be set to match the rate used in Final Cut Pro.

Setting the Sampling Rate

The sampling rate is the audio equivalent of frames per second in the video world. In essence, a sample is a discrete recording of a sound at a moment in time, and the sampling rate determines how many "moments in time" play per second. The higher the sampling rate, the more closely the sound mimics an analog waveform. In theory, a higher sampling rate produces a more accurate reproduction of the sound, but in practice, you rarely need to use a sampling rate higher than 48 kHz. The reason is simple: only the most discerning of human ears can hear the difference between a 48 kHz file and a file recorded at a higher sampling rate (dogs can hear the difference, though, so if your recording depends on having an audible dog whistle in it, go with the higher sampling rate). Note that Final Cut Pro works only in 48 kHz.

> **MORE INFO** ▶ One thing to keep in mind: A higher sampling rate does provide a more accurate reproduction of sound, but it also places a much greater strain on your computer as you edit your soundtracks. If you use a higher sampling rate, you will be able to play back fewer tracks in real time and add fewer effects to your soundtracks. With this in mind, you may need to experiment on your system to see what sampling rate works best for your editing workflow.

> In the video world, the 48 kHz sampling rate is the most common one used, so when in doubt, stick to a sampling rate of 48 kHz.

1   At the top of the Multitrack Editor, position your pointer over the Sample Rate pop-up menu, which says 48.0.

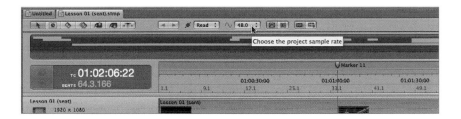

This menu controls the project's sampling rate.

2   Click and hold the menu.

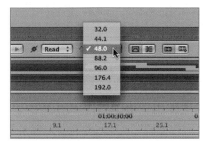

Sampling rates from 32 to 192 kHz are displayed. As you can see, Soundtrack Pro is very versatile when it comes to working with sampling rates.

NOTE ▶ You should be careful to edit at the same sampling rate as your Final Cut Pro sequence. If you choose a different sampling rate, Final Cut Pro may need to render your audio files for playback, or at the very least will need to convert them in real time as it plays the sequence, placing a greater burden on your processor.

3   Leave the sampling rate set to 48 kHz.

Working with Timecode

The timecode provides a method for identifying individual frames in a video sequence. The timecode standard is set by the Society of Motion Picture and Television Engineers (SMPTE), and it takes the form of *Hours : Minutes : Seconds : Frames.*

Soundtrack Pro is capable of reading all formats for timecode, including drop and non-drop frame. But even more important, Soundtrack Pro will let you change the initial timecode values of the sequences you are working on. This is a key feature if, for example, you are working on a small scene from a larger video sequence. Directors will often give you an edit decision list (EDL) with certain sound effects "spotted" to certain timecode values in the video. To ensure that the EDL lines up with the timecode values displayed in Soundtrack Pro, just change the initial timecode value in Soundtrack Pro to match the initial timecode value of the scene you're working on, and all of the information in your EDL will properly reflect the timecode values you see in Soundtrack Pro.

> **MORE INFO** ▶ In Final Cut Pro it is common to start timecode values at 1 hour (01:00:00:00). This standard has been accepted by the video community because it is common to put color bars and a 1 kHz test tone at the beginning of a video so the broadcast engineer can calibrate his equipment to properly play the video. There may also be a countdown lead-in added before the first frame of video. All of this information takes time, but in timecode values, you can't have a negative number. Consequently, starting the show timecode at 01:00:00:00 provides space before the first frame to add this extra information.

The project you're working on uses timecode values that start at 1 hour. Let's change that now.

1 At the top of the left pane, click the Project tab.

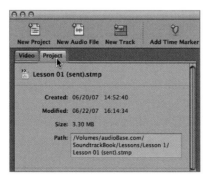

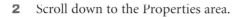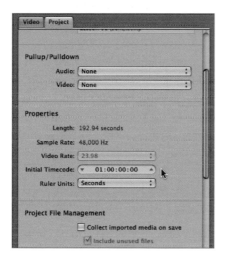

2   Scroll down to the Properties area.

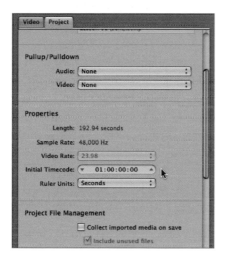

In the Properties area is an Initial Timecode setting that reads 01:00:00:00.

3   Drag down on the hours segment of the timecode value slider to set the
Initial Timecode value to 00:00:00:00.

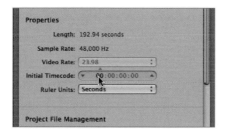

Now, the ruler along the top of the Multitrack Editor actually displays 3 seconds
(00:00:03:00) into the song when you *are* 3 seconds into the song, instead of
1 hour and 3 seconds (01:00:03:00).

Playing and Stopping Songs

Like all other audio programs, Soundtrack Pro follows certain standards for playing back and pausing songs as you work on them. For example, transport controls are located at the bottom of the workspace; they contain all the standard playback controls you're used to seeing in Final Cut Pro (plus a few others we'll explore as the book progresses). You can also toggle playback by pressing the spacebar. To get a feel for how this works, let's play the song now.

1 On your keyboard, press the Home key.

The playhead jumps to the beginning of the song.

2 In the transport controls at the bottom of the Multitrack Editor, click the Play button.

The project starts playing from the beginning and the Play button turns into a Pause button.

3 To stop playback, click the Pause button.

Playback stops. While the Play/Pause button provides a nice visual button for you to click, you'll probably prefer the next method for your everyday editing workflow.

4   Press the spacebar.

Soundtrack Pro begins playing from the playhead's last position.

5   Press the spacebar a second time.

Soundtrack Pro stops playback.

J-K-L Playback

For years Final Cut Pro editors have been using the J, K, and L keys to play projects in forward and reverse. These keys also work in Soundtrack Pro. Specifically, these keys cause Soundtrack Pro to play in reverse (J), to stop playback (K), and to play forward (L). And if that's not enough, pressing the J or L keys multiple times plays the song backward or forward at two times the normal speed, four times the normal speed, and so forth.

1   Press the L key.

Soundtrack Pro plays the song at normal playback speed.

2   Press the L key a second time.

Soundtrack Pro plays at twice the normal playback speed.

3   Press the J key.

Soundtrack Pro downgrades the playback speed once, and plays in normal speed again.

4   Press the J key a second time.

Soundtrack Pro plays at normal reverse speed.

5   Press the J key a third time.

Soundtrack Pro plays at twice the normal reverse speed.

6   Press the K key.

Soundtrack Pro stops playback.

Moving Around the Timeline

In the section above you learned some quick methods for playing projects in forward and reverse. However, if you want to jump quickly to a different part of the song, the playback controls won't help. To accomplish this task, you need to know how to position the playhead.

Positioning the Playhead

The playhead indicates the current moment of time that is playing in your project. To jump around in your project, you must move the playhead.

1 In the ruler at the top of the Multitrack Editor, click once.

The playhead moves to the clicked position. You can also click within the tracks themselves to move the playhead, but this can be dangerous as it's possible to select and accidentally move a clip if you do not click in the ruler at the top of the editor.

If need be, you can also "scrub" the playhead. When you scrub the playhead, Soundtrack Pro plays a quick, repeating section of the music under the playhead's current position. This gives you a fast preview of the sounds in that section of the project.

2 Drag the playhead's triangular handle left or right.

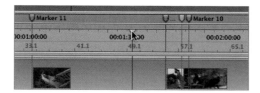

Soundtrack Pro plays a short repeating section of the song.

> **NOTE ▶** Take care to click directly on the playhead's triangular handle, or you may accidentally set a cycle region. We'll look at cycle regions in Lessons 5 and 6.

Using the Scrub Tool

The Scrub tool provides a more accurate reproduction of the sound directly under the scrubbed point, and in a very intuitive way. When you scrub, only the clip under the pointer is played. This allows you to audition clips instantly to find particular sounds.

1 Select the Scrub tool at the top of the Multitrack Editor, or press H on your keyboard.

2 Position the Scrub tool over any audio clip, and then drag left and right.

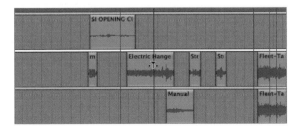

As you drag, the Scrub tool auditions the clip in a way that sounds similar to an audiotape scrubbing back and forth over the playhead. Depending on how you scrub, it might even sound like a DJ scratching a record. But the important thing to keep in mind is that only the clip you scrub will play, and all other clips will be temporarily muted.

NOTE ▶ If you scrub over a section of the Timeline that has no clips, the Scrub tool will make no sound because there's nothing directly under the pointer for it to play.

Exploring the Track Header

In the Multitrack Editor, the track header is the area of the track directly to the left of where the audio waveform is displayed. The track header contains some important controls, including volume and pan sliders, as well as Mute and Solo buttons. Let's take a look at these controls now.

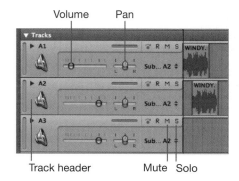

Volume and Pan

The volume and pan settings affect the loudness and left-right stereo positioning of each track in your project. These settings are your primary mix controls, used to position sounds in your audio soundscape.

1   Play the song.

2   On track A5 & A6, adjust the volume slider to hear the effect.

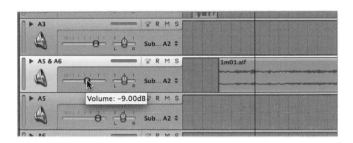

3 On the same track, adjust the pan slider to hear the effect.

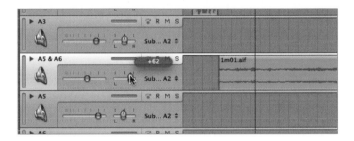

4 Once you're finished adjusting the volume and pan sliders, double-click each one.

The sliders return to their default positions. Remember this little trick, because it works to reset all sliders in Soundtrack Pro.

TIP If you need to fine-tune your volume and pan settings over time, use Soundtrack Pro envelopes. To show the envelopes, click the disclosure triangle to the left of the track name. As shown on the next page, this reveals an automation row, and you can click the envelope (the line stretching across the length of the project) to add and move envelope points. We'll look at envelopes in more detail in Lesson 7.

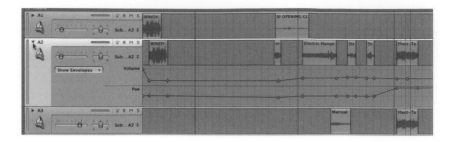

Mute and Solo

The mute and solo functions are polar opposites of each other. Mute temporarily disables the playback of any muted track, while solo temporarily disables the playback of any track that is not solo'd.

1   Play the project.

2   On track A5 & A6, click the Mute button.

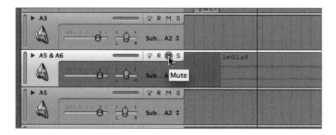

You can no longer hear the track, and the track itself is grayed out or muted.

3   Click the Mute button again to enable playback of the track.

4   On track A5 & A6, click the Solo button.

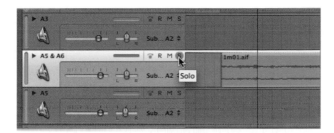

You can now hear only the solo'd track, and all the rest of the tracks are grayed out.

5   Click the Solo button again to allow all tracks to play.

Returning to Final Cut Pro

After you've finished your edits in Soundtrack Pro, you need to get the finished audio back into Final Cut Pro. Whether your edits are light (as in the ones you've made in this lesson) or heavy (as in the ones you'll make in future lessons), the process is the same: Bounce out a finished version of your Soundtrack Pro project, and add it to your Final Cut Pro sequence.

> **NOTE** ▶ Soundtrack Pro 2 introduced a new feature called "Conform," which is designed to synchronize changes made to a Final Cut Pro project with an associated Soundtrack Pro project. Conform is discussed in detail by Apple lead trainer Steve Martin in Lesson 10.

Exporting Your Song

Whether you're exporting your project to finish a roundtrip with Final Cut Pro or creating a master copy to archive on DVD, publish to the Internet, or place on an audio CD, the process of exporting is more or less the same.

1   From the File menu, choose Export (Command-E).

The Export dialog drops down from the title bar. There are a lot of menus in this dialog, and we'll discuss each one in sequence as these steps progress. To start, let's name the file and select a save folder.

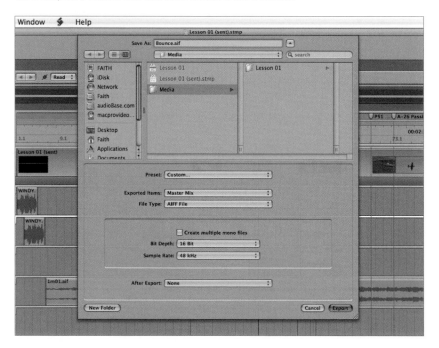

NOTE ► By default, Soundtrack Pro bounces from the beginning of the song to the red marker at the end of your project (end-of-song markers are discussed in Lesson 8). However, there is one exception to this rule: If you've defined a cycle region in your project, Soundtrack Pro exports only the portion of the project between the In and Out points that define the cycle region (cycle regions are discussed in detail in Lessons 5 and 6).

2 Navigate to the folder where you'd like to save the file, and then name the file *Bounce* in the Save As field.

3 Leave the Presets menu set to Custom.

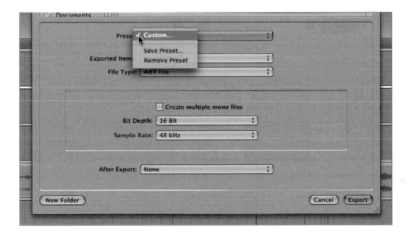

The other options in the menu can be used to store a collection of export settings as defined by the pop-up menus lower in the Export dialog. If you find yourself often exporting files using the exact same settings, it can pay in spades to take a moment and set up a preset. You'll save time down the road by not having to make selections from the menus every time you export.

4 From the Exported Items menu, choose Master Mix.

Pay attention to the other settings in this dialog, as they can come in handy if, for example, you need to send a "tracked out" version of the project to an editor that is not using Soundtrack Pro. For example, if you choose All Tracks, Busses, and Submixes in the Exported Items menu, Soundtrack Pro creates exported files for each individual track, bus, and submix that other editors can import into their digital audio workstations for further editing.

5 From the File Type menu, choose AIFF File.

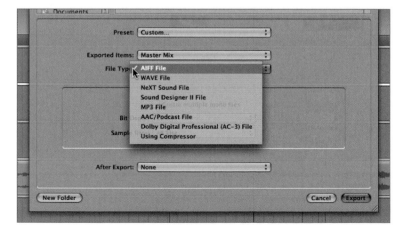

AIFF is the audio file type commonly used on Apple computers. Notice there are also several compressed formats to choose from, including MP3, AAC, and Dolby Digital AC-3 files, which are used in DVD-Video and digital cable television.

NOTE ▶ The export options contained in the area directly below the File Type menu will change depending on the type of file you export.

6   Leave the bit depth at 16 Bit and the sample rate at 48 kHz.

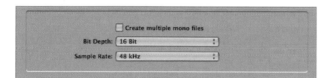

These are the same bit depth and sample rate as the original Final Cut Pro sequence, so there's no need to change them now.

7   From the After Export menu, choose "Send files to Final Cut Pro sequence."

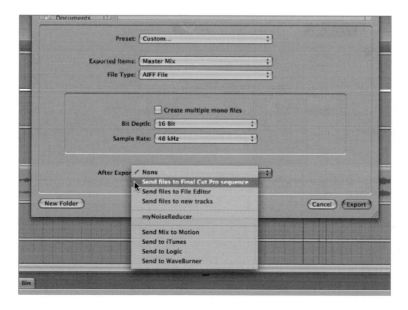

This is where the magic really happens. In the next several steps, the exported audio will be automatically imported back into a Final Cut Pro sequence so you can seamlessly continue the video portion of your editing.

8   Click the Export button.

This step can take a few minutes, as your computer will now open the original Final Cut Pro sequence and prepare to import the new audio. When the computer is ready, an Import XML dialog appears in Final Cut Pro.

NOTE ▶ If Final Cut Pro is closed when you initiate this action, it will not open the sequence for you. For the example above, the original sequence was left open during this lesson. But if the original project is not open, you will need to open it in Final Cut Pro before initiating the step above.

9   From the Destination menu in the Import XML dialog, choose 01-Begin, and then click OK.

A new sequence is created in the Final Cut Pro Browser, and the sequence is automatically given the same name as your exported audio file. But it contains a whole lot more than just your finished audio.

10   In the Browser, open the *Bounce* sequence.

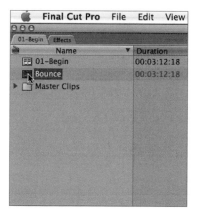

The *Bounce* sequence Timeline opens. At the top of the audio area there are two tracks enabled, and these two tracks contain your finished audio file. Below those two tracks are all the component audio clips from the original Final Cut Pro sequence, but they are muted. If you need to redo the audio at any point, all the building blocks are still available to you for yet another roundtrip. Now that's a cool feature!

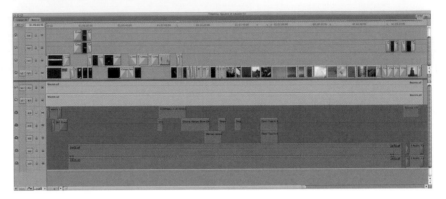

Lesson Review

1. How do you send a sequence from Final Cut Pro to Soundtrack Pro?

2. True or false: All tabs must remain in their original panes and cannot be moved.

3. What do the J, K, and L keys do?

4. What does the Scrub tool do?

5. When you export files and choose the "Send files to Final Cut Pro sequence" command, what happens?

Answers

1. Select the sequence in Final Cut Pro's Browser, then choose File > Send To > Soundtrack Pro Multitrack Project.

2. False. You can move tabs to different panes, or even drag them out of panes to create floating windows.

3. J plays the song in reverse, K stops playback, and L plays the song forward. Pressing J or L multiple times increases the playback rate in both reverse and forward.

4. The Scrub tool lets you audition the sound of individual clips in your project.

5. Soundtrack Pro exports the file, opens Final Cut Pro if it's not already running, and creates a sequence with the same name as the exported audio file. Better still, if the original Final Cut Pro project is already open in FCP, you can choose it from the Destination pop-up menu so that all of the video and audio clips from the original sequence you sent to Soundtrack Pro will be added to the new sequence. The original video clips will be added to the tracks above the exported Soundtrack Pro audio clips, and the original audio clips are added to muted tracks beneath.

2

Lesson Files	APTS-SoundtrackPro > Lesson 02 > 02 Begin.fcp
Time	This lesson takes approximately 60 minutes to complete.
Goals	Send audio clips from Final Cut Pro to Soundtrack Pro
	Explore zoom techniques
	Edit audio files at the sample level
	Fix pops and clicks
	Reduce noise in an audio file
	Use Soundtrack Pro scripts

Fixing Audio Files

With today's digital video cameras, creating high-quality visual images is easier than ever. All you need is good lighting and a camcorder.

However, if you're like most people shooting digital video, you're probably relying on the camera's built-in microphone to record your scene's audio. In many ways, this makes sense. Recording the audio directly onto the same tape or card that is storing the video ensures that the audio and video remain in sync, making them easy to edit once you bring the media into Final Cut Pro. And the easiest way to record the sound onto the same tape is to use the built-in microphone.

But using a camera's built-in microphone has disadvantages. For example, the microphone is very close to the camera motors that spin the tape as you record your scene, and because of this, it's common to hear motor noise in the background. Compounding this effect, the camera mic is often far from the focus of the scene's action, so the sound of the character's voice is more distant, and the sound of the room's noise is closer. Additionally, the microphones in cameras are subject to wind noise, and sometimes spotty analog-to-digital conversions can result in pops and clicks in your final recording.

A good microphone can minimize these problems, and it's always important to try to record the best sound possible while shooting. But even with the best equipment, there are still obstacles that can keep a recording from sounding as good as it should. Fortunately, Soundtrack Pro makes it easy to leap over them.

In this lesson, you will begin exploring Soundtrack Pro's audio restoration and cleanup functions. Specifically, you'll learn how to remove pops and clicks, decrease background noise, and clean those audio files so that they are sonically pristine.

Opening a Sequence in Final Cut Pro

Soundtrack Pro is more than just an audio postproduction tool; it's an audio postproduction tool that is meant to work with Final Cut Pro. In fact, Sound-track Pro 2 has been designed from the ground up to work seamlessly with Apple's flagship video editing program, and it's now easier than ever to swap files between the two programs. Let's examine this tight integration by opening a sequence in Final Cut Pro.

1   From the lesson files that came with this book, locate the Lesson 02 folder and choose the **02 Begin.fcp** file to open it in Final Cut Pro.

  NOTE ▶ If you're not already familiar with the basic functions of Final Cut Pro, you can still follow along with this section to play and send video sequences to Soundtrack Pro.

  A sequence opens in Final Cut Pro.

2   Press the spacebar to play the sequence. Listen closely to the audio as you watch the picture to get a feel for the media you will be working with. Listen for any pops, hums, noise, or other unsavory artifacts that may be in the sound.

Opening Audio Files from Final Cut Pro

You probably noticed a big problem with clip **0006OE.mov**, which begins at the first marker, 58 seconds into the sequence. This file has several annoying clicks in it. Clicks almost always occur when analog-to-digital converters make mistakes in the conversion process (analog-to-digital, or AD, converters transform the natural sounds you hear into digital information that a computer can edit).

You may also have noticed a great deal of noise in the signal, and even some high-pitched squeals in a few of the clips that may have come from the camera itself, or an air conditioning unit close to the microphone, or who knows what.

The important point is that all these extraneous sounds need to be removed from the signal. We'll start with those very noticeable pops and clicks in clip **0006OE.mov**.

1   In the Final Cut Pro sequence, Control-click the Timecode ruler and choose Example 1 from the shortcut menu.

The playhead jumps to the first marker in the sequence, which sits at the beginning of clip **0006OE.mov**.

2   Control-click clip **0006OE.mov** and choose Send To > Soundtrack Pro
Audio File Project from the shortcut menu.

A Save dialog appears.

To send the file to Soundtrack Pro, you need to create a new Soundtrack
Pro (.stap) file. In the future, both Soundtrack Pro and Final Cut Pro will
need to reference this file, so make sure that you put it into a folder you
will remember. For now, you'll put it in a new folder inside the Lesson 02
folder.

NOTE ▶ By now you should have copied this book's media files to your
computer. If you are running the files directly from the DVD that came
with this book, you will not be able to follow along. For more information
about copying the source files to your computer, see "Getting Started."

3   In the Save dialog, navigate to the Lesson 02 folder on your hard disk.

4   In the lower-left corner of the Save dialog, click the New Folder button.

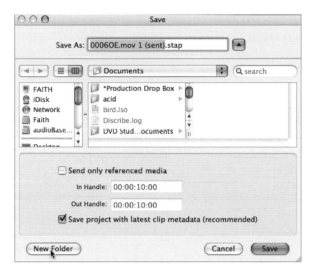

A dialog opens and asks you to name the new folder.

5 Name the folder *Soundtrack Files* and click the Create button.

A new folder is created in the Lesson 02 folder.

At this point, you have a decision to make. Notice that the Save As field of the Save dialog has been filled with a default name that matches the name of the clip in Final Cut Pro's Timeline. You can choose to either keep this default name or supply a new one. For most situations, it's best to keep the default name so that when you come back to a project after the passage of several days, or even several hours, you can tell which Soundtrack Pro file is associated with which clip in your Timeline.

6 In the Save dialog, click the Save button.

The audio clip opens in Soundtrack Pro.

▶ **Opening a File from Logic Pro**

If you're producing music in Logic Pro, Soundtrack Pro—with it's advanced audio-cleanup tools—can be used as a companion to Logic. Especially in home studios, creaks and pops of the house settling, air conditioning noise, or even a car idling outside can contaminate acoustic recordings. To correct these problems, the techniques for fixing audio files discussed in this lesson are just as applicable to cleaning up musical tracks recorded in Logic.

To bring an audio file from Logic into Soundtrack Pro, you must first configure Soundtrack Pro as Logic's external sample editor.

1   In Logic Pro choose Logic Pro > Preferences > Audio.

2   Click the Sample Editor tab.

3   Beneath the External Sample Editor section, click the Set button and choose Soundtrack Pro in your Applications folder.

4   Once Soundtrack Pro is set as Logic's external sample editor, in Logic's Arrange window, select the region you want to fix and choose Options > Audio > Open in Soundtrack Pro.

Now you can fix your audio in Soundtrack Pro using the techniques that follow in this lesson.

Exploring the File Editor Project View

The preceding lesson introduced Soundtrack Pro's workspace, and specifically the Multitrack Editor, which displays several audio tracks at the same time. When you open an audio file in Soundtrack, the workspace looks a bit different: You see only the audio file's channels in the workspace. Because the audio file you just opened is a mono file, you currently see only one audio channel. However, don't be fooled, because audio files can also contain two channels (stereo), or even more. For example, a 5.1 surround audio file would have six channels of audio, and each of those channels would be visible in the File Editor project view.

File Editor project view

1   To play the file, click the Play button in the transport controls at the bottom of the File Editor project view, or press the spacebar.

The Play button becomes a Pause button.

2   To stop playback, click the Pause button, or press the spacebar a second time.

About the Waveform Display

By default, the waveform display opens in the File Editor project view. This view shows you the amplitude, or volume, of the various parts of the file—that's all a waveform does. (A waveform is a common way to look at sound, even in applications such as Final Cut Pro or Motion.) Although Soundtrack Pro does provide a special view that shows you frequency information for the file, we'll leave that view for the next lesson and concentrate solely on the waveform display for now.

Because we are looking at the amplitude of the audio file, and because audio amplitude is most commonly measured in decibels (dB), you'll change the waveform display's scale so that it measures amplitude in decibels. The new scale will then also match the meters on the plug-ins that come with Soundtrack Pro. This process will be particularly important later in this lesson when we discuss how to normalize (adjust the gain of) audio files, so follow the next steps closely.

1   Look at the amplitude scale on the left edge of the waveform display.

Amplitude scale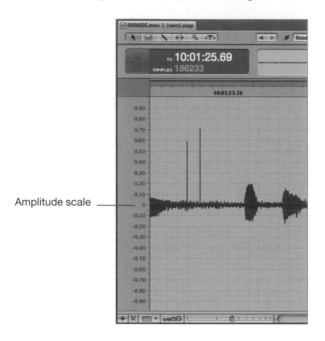

At the moment, this scale shows the amplitude with level indicators linearly spread from 0 to plus or minus 1. Let's change that to the more common decibel scale.

2   Control-click the amplitude scale.

A shortcut menu appears.

3   From the shortcut menu, choose Decibels.

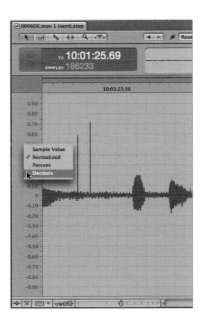

The scale changes to decibels (dB). You can now see, for example, that the loudest sound in this file peaks at approximately –3 dB.

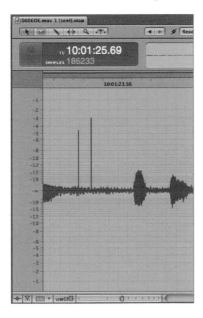

Positioning the Playhead

As the audio file plays, the playhead travels from left to right across the screen. You can reposition the playhead to any point in the audio file and then begin playback from that point.

1   Click the waveform close to the beginning of the file on the left side of the Timeline.

The playhead jumps to the point where you clicked.

Zooming and Scrolling

As you played the file, you heard three obvious clicks. In fact, you don't even need to play the file to know that the file contains these clicks—they are clearly represented in the file's waveform as three upward spikes. You'll take a closer look at these little trouble spots by zooming in on the first click.

1   Position the playhead on the first pop in the wave by clicking directly on top of it.

By placing the playhead directly on the pop, you can more easily zoom in to see this pop in detail. The playhead acts as a sort of "marker" that lets you easily locate the pop after you've zoomed in on the waveform.

2   Press Shift-Z.

Notice that the entire waveform now fits snuggly within the waveform display. Shift-Z is a handy key command to keep in mind, and it works not only in Soundtrack Pro but also in Final Cut Pro. However, you are still not zoomed in quite enough to examine the first pop, so now try a different zooming technique.

3   On the scroll bar at the bottom of the File Editor project view, grab the right handle and drag it toward the left.

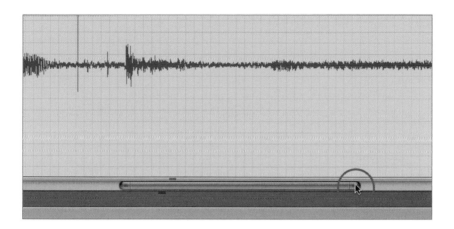

The File Editor zooms in on the wave.

However, as you drag, you may notice that the playhead disappears off the left edge of the screen. Fortunately, there's an easy way to center your zooming and get that important playhead back into view. At the lower left of the File Editor project view is a dedicated Zoom control that automatically centers your zooming on the playhead.

4   Drag the Zoom control all the way to the left to zoom in on the playhead.

Zoom control

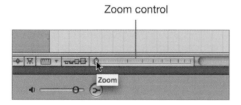

NOTE ▶ Key commands make zooming fast and easy. To zoom in press Command-= (equals sign) and to zoom out press Command-– (minus sign).

Using the Global Waveform View

Unless you positioned the pointer exactly on the first click, you've probably zoomed in so close that the click is no longer visible in the waveform display. That's a problem, because it is this click that you want to focus on. We'll use a few little tricks to get that click into view.

At the top of the File Editor project view is the Global Waveform view, which displays important information about your file. First and foremost, the overview displays the audio file's waveform from the very first sample in the waveform to the very last—in other words, the overview always shows you the entire audio file. The Global Waveform view also displays the playhead, which looks like a yellow triangle pointing down from the top of the overview.

The third item in the Global Waveform view is a blue visible area rectangle placed over the waveform. This rectangle shows you which part of the waveform you are looking at in the main waveform display. When you are zoomed in on the waveform, you can drag the rectangle in the overview to quickly jump to a different place in the audio file.

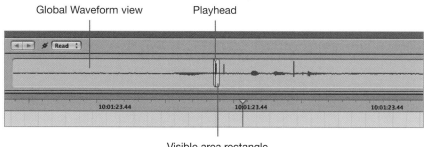

1   Grab the blue visible area rectangle and drag it so it is centered on the first click in the audio file.

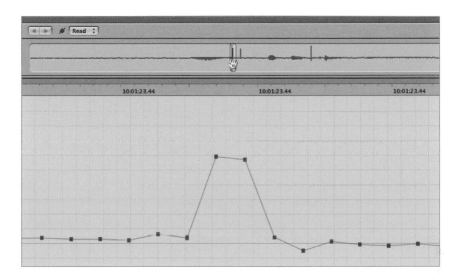

This step can be difficult to accomplish because you are zoomed in to the maximum degree. Get as close as you can by dragging, and then you'll use the right or left arrow buttons to the right of the scroll bar to refine your selection by clicking through the wave left or right.

2 To the right of the scroll bar, click the left or right arrow buttons until you have the click centered on your screen.

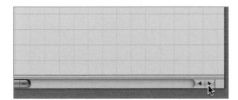

To ensure that you don't lose the click by accidentally zooming, you can take the precautionary step of centering the playhead directly on the click. If you scroll or zoom out, you can then use the Zoom control (or press Z) to quickly zoom back in on the click.

3   In the waveform display, click directly on the pop in the waveform to
center the playhead on it.

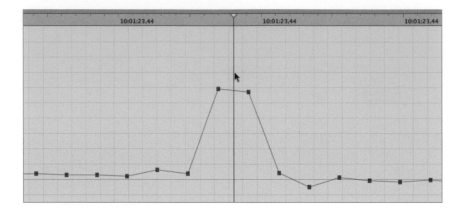

Redrawing Waveforms

At this point, you are looking at the file in the most microscopic view possible.
In fact, you've zoomed all the way down to the sample level: Each individual
dot, or node, you see on the line is an individual sample in this audio file. In a
moment, you are going to edit some of these samples by hand. Because you
can see and edit the individual samples in an audio file, Soundtrack Pro is
classified as a sample-accurate audio editor, and that's an important distinc-
tion when you need to restore and clean up audio files.

Note that when you edit files using the technique shown here, you are actually
editing the volume of the distinct samples—not the "sound" of the samples
themselves. However, that's good enough for fixing pops and clicks. Of course,
the sound of the sample may be garbled by poor AD conversion, but that's
fine. Every second of the audio file you are editing contains 48,000 samples,
so even if one or two samples per second are sonically corrupted, your ear
won't hear them. You will, however, hear the dramatic *pop* that occurs in a

few samples that are far too loud, and that's the pop that you will remove in the next steps.

1   From the waveform editing tools, grab the Sample Edit tool (also called the Pencil tool), or press P.

2   Drag a straight horizontal line over the click in the audio file, or drag each of the click nodes down to level out the waveform.

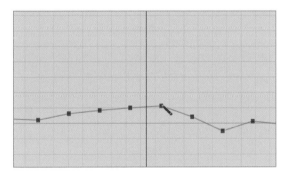

Presto chango! The click is gone.

The click resulted from a dramatic spike in volume between one sample and the next. On a mechanical level, a sudden spike in volume causes your playback speakers to very quickly pop in and out, which in turn causes clicks like the one you heard before. Now see if this fix worked.

3   Zoom out on the waveform so you can play back the file with enough lead time to hear if the click is gone.

4   Move the playhead to a position before the point where the click used to be.

5   Play the file.

The first click in the file is gone, but two clicks remain. You can follow the preceding steps to remove those final two clicks by hand, or you can use a faster technique, detailed in the next section. But first, switch back to the Selection tool so you don't accidentally edit this file's samples during the next steps.

6   From the waveform editing tools, select the Selection tool, or press A.

Analyzing an Audio File

The preceding steps were time consuming. Happily, there's a much faster and easier way to remove pops and clicks from an audio file. In fact, Soundtrack Pro can analyze an audio file to remove several common problems: not only pops and clicks, but also power-line hum (also called ground-loop hum), DC offset, phase problems, and clipped signals. In this section, you'll analyze the file for clicks and pops only, but the process is the same for each of the other problems listed here.

▶   **Clicks and pops:** Clicks and pops occur when a few samples in the audio file dramatically spike in volume, causing the speakers to momentarily pop forward, creating a clicking sound.

▶   **Power-line hum:** Power-line hum is caused by a ground loop, where electricity feeds back through the grounding wire to create an audible hum at either 59.97 Hz (in NTSC countries, where the power cycles at 59.97 Hz) or 50 Hz (in PAL countries, where the electrical power cycles at 50 Hz).

Power-line hum can also occur when power lines are cabled close to unshielded audio cables.

▶ **DC offset:** DC offset (or direct current offset) is immediately noticeable because the waveform does not cycle around its 0 axis, but is instead off-set, or slightly raised from the 0 axis. Although DC offset is technically not audible, it does have dramatic implications when you want to compress your audio file: for example, when you want to create an AC-3 file for a DVD-Video project. It also decreases the dynamic range available to your audio file.

▶ **Phase problems:** Phase problems occur in stereo files when the waveforms in the left and right channels are slightly offset from each other. This effect causes the left speaker to push as the right speaker pulls. Slight phase problems can cause sounds to seem to swirl back and forth between speakers, while more dramatic phase problems can cause certain frequencies to drop out altogether from the playback sound.

▶ **Clipped signal:** A clipped signal, also called digital distortion, occurs when a sound is recorded with the volume too high for the digital record-ing device: for example, when a sound is recorded with the volume above 0 dB. A clipped signal looks like a flattened waveform. Clipped sound gets its name because this flattened waveform looks like somebody has taken digital scissors and clipped the tops off the peaks in the wave.

1 In the left pane of the workspace, click the Analysis tab.

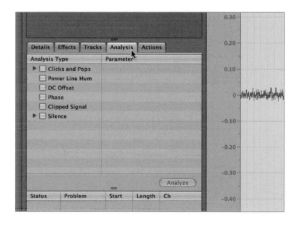

2   Click the Clicks and Pops checkbox to select it.

If desired, you can also click the checkboxes beside the other common audio problems, and Soundtrack Pro will analyze the file for these problems, too.

3   Click the disclosure triangle next to the Clicks and Pops checkbox.

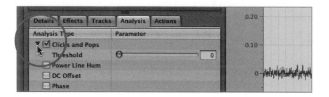

The Threshold slider is revealed. The Threshold slider is used to set the sensitivity of the Clicks and Pops analysis. Specifically, Soundtrack Pro will look only for Clicks and Pops that are above the threshold that you set.

The slider's scale covers a range from 0 to 100. Looking at the clicks in this file, you can see that they are all above the halfway mark on the amplitude scale, while all the other sounds are quite a bit lower than halfway up the amplitude scale, so let's designate a threshold setting of 50.

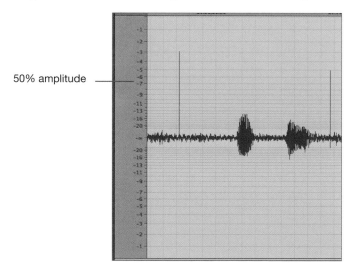

50% amplitude

4   Move the Clicks and Pops Threshold slider to set a value of 50.

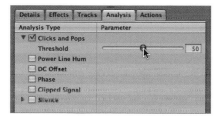

5   On the Analysis tab, click the Analyze button.

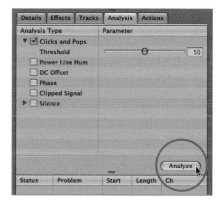

In the waveform display, Soundtrack Pro highlights two potential problem areas in red.

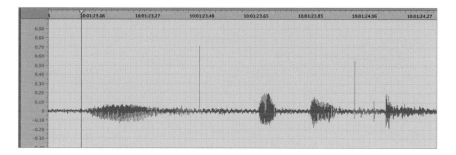

On the Analysis tab, these problem areas are displayed in the Analysis Results list. However, Soundtrack Pro has only analyzed the file at this point, so the problems have not been fixed. Move on to the next section to learn how to fix this file.

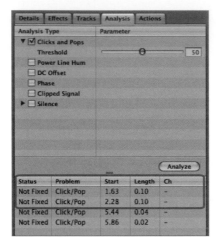

Zooming In on Problems

If you need a better view of a problem, Soundtrack Pro has a handy feature that lets you temporarily zoom in and check out the problem in detail.

1   In the Analysis Results list, click the first problem to select it.

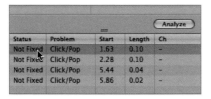

In the waveform display, only the first problem area is now highlighted in red.

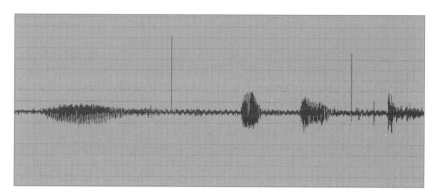

2 At the bottom of the Analysis tab, click and hold the Magnify button.

Status	Problem	Start	Length	Ch
Not Fixed	Click/Pop	1.63	0.10	–
Not Fixed	Click/Pop	2.28	0.10	–
Not Fixed	Click/Pop	5.44	0.04	–
Not Fixed	Click/Pop	5.86	0.02	–

Analyze

Clear Fixed   Fix All   Fix

While the button is held, the File Editor temporarily zooms in to show the problem in detail.

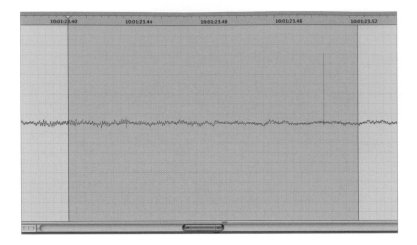

3   Release the Magnify button.

The waveform display returns to the previous zoom level.

Fixing the Problems Soundtrack Pro Finds

When you analyze an audio file, Soundtrack Pro only shows you where the problem areas are. It's up to you to decide whether these areas really are problems and, if so, whether you need to fix them. You'll now fix your file's problems one by one.

1   Make sure that the first problem is still selected in the Analysis Results list. Then, at the lower right of the Analysis tab, click the Fix button.

A progress indicator drops down from the Soundtrack Pro title bar and updates you as the fix progresses.

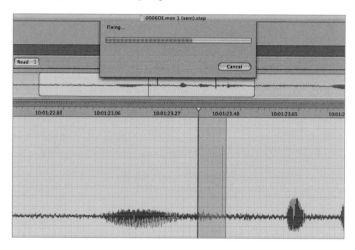

After Soundtrack Pro finishes fixing the click, notice that the click is gone from the waveform and the Status column of the Analysis Results list now shows the problem as Fixed.

Status	Problem	Start	Length	Ch
Fixed	Click/Pop	1.63	0.10	–
Not Fixed	Click/Pop	2.28	0.10	–
Not Fixed	Click/Pop	5.44	0.04	–

2   In the lower-right corner of the Analysis tab, click the Fix All button.

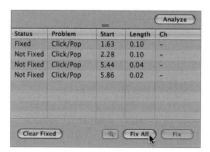

Status	Problem	Start	Length	Ch
Fixed	Click/Pop	1.63	0.10	–
Not Fixed	Click/Pop	2.28	0.10	–
Not Fixed	Click/Pop	5.44	0.04	–
Not Fixed	Click/Pop	5.86	0.02	–

Soundtrack Pro fixes all of the remaining pops.

Working with Actions

In the last few exercises you removed some pops and clicks from an audio file, and along the way you learned how to analyze an audio file to fix some common problems that can occur in video shoots. While Soundtrack Pro's ability to perform this type of audio restoration and repair is pretty cool, it pales in comparison to the capabilities of the feature you will learn about next: actions.

What Are Actions?

Actions are the core of Soundtrack Pro's audio editing foundation, and they are unique to this program: No other digital audio workstation (DAW) on the market today handles nondestructive editing as elegantly as Soundtrack Pro. To understand why, take a moment to consider the concept of nondestructive audio editing.

The term *nondestructive editing* is used to classify any edit you perform that does not change the source audio file. Indeed, most of today's popular DAWs (such as Apple Logic Pro) are classified as nondestructive audio editors because all the editing information is stored in the song project file you are working on, while the source file on your hard disk is never changed in any way. This is a great feature, because at any time you can reuse that source audio file without the changes you made to it in your DAW. On the flip side, if you're in another application and you do want to hear the changes you made to the file, you must first bounce (or render) the file to create a new audio file.

Soundtrack Pro takes the concept of nondestructive audio editing to the next level, using actions. When you make changes to an audio file in Soundtrack Pro and then save the file, the changes are stored in the file itself as metadata (extra information that some programs can read). Any program that understands how to interpret this special metadata will apply these changes, and programs that don't understand the metadata will ignore the changes.

Furthermore, at any time you can reopen the file in Soundtrack Pro and simply remove the applied actions. Let's take a look now at how actions work.

1   In the left pane of the workspace, click the Actions tab.

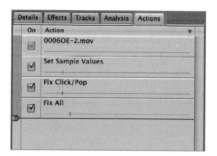

Seven actions are currently listed under the source audio file on this tab: one Set Sample Values action and two Fix Click/Pop actions. These are the edits you performed in the last few exercises. Beside each of these actions is a checkbox.

NOTE ▶ If you were not precise while using the Pencil tool earlier in this lesson, or if you did a bit of experimenting outside the lessons, you may see more Set Sample Values actions than are listed in the figure.

2   Deselect the checkbox to the left of the second Fix Click/Pop action.

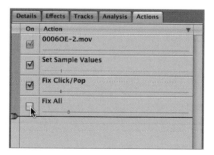

Notice in the waveform display that the third click is now back in the audio file.

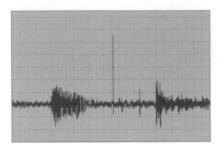

3   Toggle the Fix Click/Pop action on again to remove the click from the file.

Where's My Action?

Actions are powerful and versatile. For example, you can apply actions to an entire file or to only certain parts of the audio file, depending on the editing situation at hand.

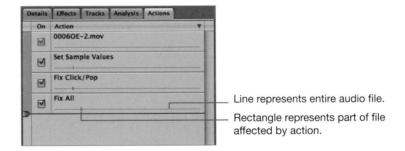

Line represents entire audio file.

Rectangle represents part of file affected by action.

In the case of the third action in our list, notice that there is a green line under the name of each Fix Click/Pop action, and a little box about halfway along the green line. The line itself represents the entire audio file, while the little box represents the portion of the file to which the action has been applied. To see how the display changes, let's apply an action to the entire file.

1   In the File Editor, click somewhere on the waveform to ensure that the File Editor is the active editing window and can thus accept keyboard input.

2   Press Command-A to select the entire audio file.

3   On the main menu bar, click Process.

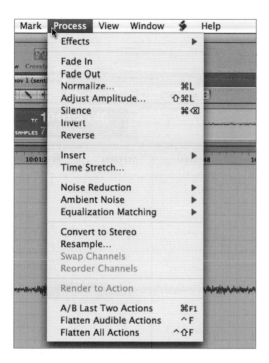

Before continuing, take a moment to look at the options in this menu. Each represents a type of action you can perform on this audio file. As you can see, you have many choices.

4   Choose the Normalize option.

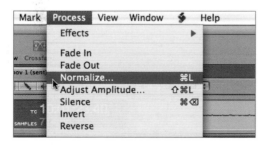

The Normalize dialog drops down from Soundtrack Pro's title bar. This dialog contains the normalization level controls.

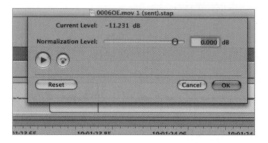

Normalization is a process that adjusts the peak volume of an audio file to a set level. The level you choose depends on the type of audio you are working on and its intended delivery medium. For example, for audio destined for an audio CD, you would commonly normalize to 0 dB to make the audio as loud as possible without clipping it. For audio destined for television broadcast, you would normalize to the industry-recognized peak level of –6 dB.

5   Set the Normalization Level value to –6 dB and click OK.

In the File Editor project view, the waveform grows, indicating that the volume has become louder.

6   Play the file to hear how normalization has affected its volume.

7   On the Actions tab, look at the Actions list.

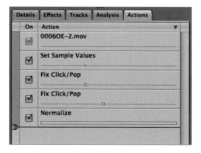

Notice that the box under the Normalize action covers the entire green line, indicating that the entire file has been normalized, while the boxes under the Fix Click/Pop actions cover only a small part of the green line, indicating that those actions affect only a small part of the audio file. Pretty cool stuff.

Putting Your Actions in Order

Because actions offer an entirely nondestructive way to work with audio files, you can reorder actions at will without worrying about destroying or permanently altering your original source audio file. However, when reordering actions, you must keep in mind that actions affect an audio file from top to bottom in the Actions list. Depending on the type of actions used, order can have a dramatic effect on the sound of your audio file.

1   Drag the Normalize action to the top of the Actions list.

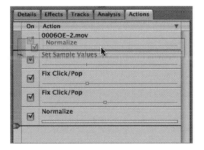

In the waveform display, the waveform updates and grows smaller, not larger as it did when the Normalize action appeared at the end of the list. This behavior occurs because Soundtrack Pro is now normalizing to the peak level of the clicks and pops in the file, instead of to the peak level of the normal sounds in the file *after* the clicks and pops have been removed. Darn!

Deleting Actions

The Normalize action graphically demonstrates how the order of your actions affects the file's sound, but you don't need this action in your file, because you'll be adjusting the volume in a later lesson, so you'll now remove the action.

1   In the Actions list, Control-click the Normalize action.

2   From the shortcut menu that appears, choose Delete "Normalize."

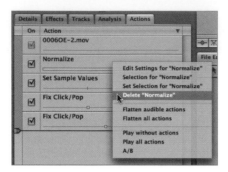

The Normalize action is deleted from the Actions list.

NOTE ▶ You can also select the action and press Delete to remove it from the Actions list.

Reducing Noise

Noise is a problem that plagues most video productions, and it can make an otherwise good production seem amateurish. Fortunately, Soundtrack Pro has excellent noise reduction features built in. But before getting into the nitty-gritty of reducing noise, take a moment to examine what, exactly, noise is.

Exploring Noise

The human ear has a natural noise-cancellation circuit built in. If you take a moment to really listen to the room around you, you'll hear all sorts of strange hissing noises and other aural oddities caused by sounds reflecting around you, but most of the time, your ear (in combination with your brain) blocks out this background noise so that you can concentrate on more important sounds (such as the rustle of the leopard about to leap out of the jungle or the voice of the person across the table from you in a restaurant).

Effective video focuses the viewer's attention on the story, and consequently it is important to decrease the volume of unimportant sounds in relation to important ones, such as the voices of the characters speaking onscreen. In essence, the audio engineer must act as the noise-canceling circuit that naturally occurs in all of us, ensuring that only the important information gets through, and nothing more. Let's listen to some noise to get a feel for this.

1 In the File Editor project view, scroll so that the beginning of the audio file can be seen.

2 Select the "silent" part at the beginning of the audio file.

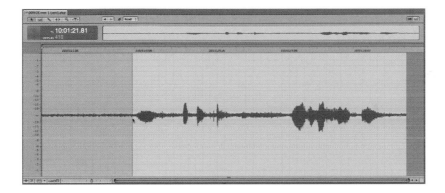

This part is not true silence, but it is a section where none of the characters are speaking.

3 At the bottom of the File Editor project view, make sure that the Cycle button is turned on.

The Cycle button causes the selected portion of the audio file to repeat continuously, which makes it easier to listen to the sound you've selected.

4 Click the Play button and listen carefully.

Although this part of the file contains a very small bit of ambient sound, most of what you are hearing is noise. There even seems to be a whirring sound, perhaps coming from the spinning of the camera motors or from some piece of equipment in the room near the microphone. Whatever the cause of the noise, it is important that you make it as quiet as possible in relation to the spoken dialogue, which naturally should be the focus of this scene.

NOTE ▶ There is a big difference between ambient noise and just plain old noise. Ambient noise is the sound of people talking in the background of the café, or the sound of cars and buses passing by on the street outside. It is not the hissy sound of the noise discussed here. Don't let anyone tell you that such hisses are ambient noise that should be included in the audio file. Be careful about what you consider to be ambient noise on the file, and make sure that it is indeed ambient sound and not just plain old noise.

Setting a Noise Print

Before Soundtrack Pro can reduce the noise from a file, you need to tell it what, in fact, the noise in the file sounds like. To do this, you must set the noise print. At a fundamental level, a noise print is sort of like a fingerprint of the noise in a file: It is the unique frequency spectrum of the background noise that you will later reduce. To use a video analogy, the noise print functions much the same as the key color selected when pulling a blue or green screen—the color you select is the base for the colors removed. Similarly, the noise print is the base for the frequencies that are removed.

As long as you've been careful to avoid selecting any of the important sounds in the file (such as the sound of the people talking), you can be confident that the sound you have selected is indeed only noise. You can now set the selection you made at the beginning of the audio file as your noise print.

1 From the Process menu, choose Noise Reduction > Set Noise Print.

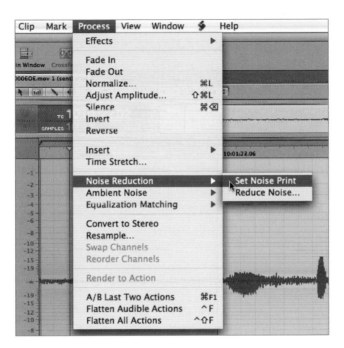

Soundtrack Pro sets the selected audio as the noise print for the file.

Opening the Reduce Noise Dialog

Reducing noise is more of an art than a science, and it takes a bit of trial and error to get it right. If you are too aggressive in your noise reduction settings, you risk making your audio sound tinny, as if it were playing out of an empty soup can—and let's face it: nobody wants to listen to that. However, if you're not aggressive enough in your settings, the noise will continue to play a prominent part in your audio file. The secret is to balance your settings to remove as much noise as possible without dramatically altering the sound of the important elements in the audio file.

While trial and error is ultimately the only way to get acceptable noise reduction, there are nonetheless a few techniques that you can use to guide your settings. You have already set your noise print, so now you can experiment with reducing the noise from this file.

1   From the Process menu, choose Noise Reduction > Reduce Noise.

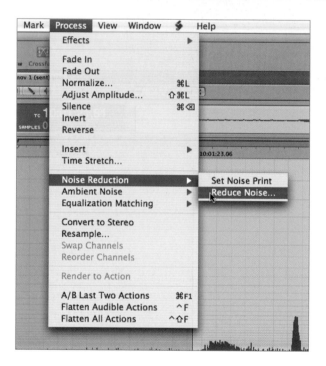

The Reduce Noise dialog appears onscreen. It contains Noise Threshold, Reduction, and Tone Control settings that combine to help you get the noise out of the file. You'll explore each of these controls in the following sections.

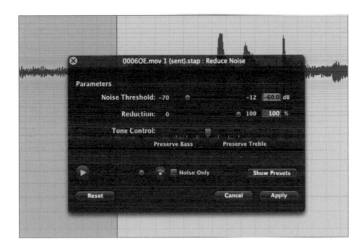

Setting a Noise Threshold

The Noise Threshold setting is at the top of the Reduce Noise dialog, and it's there for good reason: Setting the correct threshold is the single most important task in this window. Let's play the file, and then set the threshold.

1   Click the Play button.

Soundtrack Pro begins cycle playback of the selected area at the beginning of the file. Soundtrack Pro is now playing the selected audio through the Reduce Noise dialog, and you may notice that the noise now sounds a bit tinny. This is because the default Noise Threshold setting of –60 dB is a bit too aggressive.

2   As the selection plays, refer to the audio level meters on the Meters tab in the right pane.

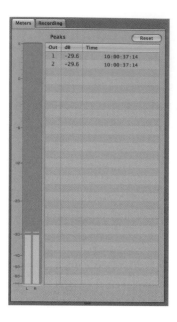

Notice that the sound of this noise peaks at around −32 dB. This value can be considered the "noise floor" of the audio file: In other words, this is the threshold below which there is noise and above which there is clean audio. This value gives you a pretty good indication of where to start experimenting with the Noise Threshold setting.

3   In the Reduce Noise dialog, set the Noise Threshold value to approximately −32 dB.

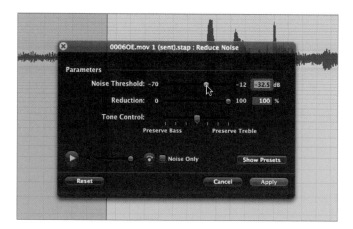

As you reduce the Noise Threshold value, notice that the sound becomes much less tinny. That's good.

Bypassing Noise Reduction to Hear Your Original Sound

As you continue to experiment with noise reduction, it is important that you once in a while toggle back to the original sound so you can judge how your noise reduction settings are affecting the audio file. The Reduce Noise dialog has a button that lets you do just that: the Preview Effect Bypass button, usually just called the Bypass button.

1   As the selection plays, click the Bypass button located to the right of the volume slider in the Reduce Noise dialog.

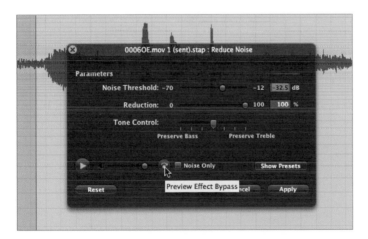

The original sound of the selection bypasses the Reduce Noise plug-in and plays.

2   Click the Bypass button again to disable its function.

You now hear the effect of the Noise Threshold setting—a pretty dramatic change!

Adjusting the Noise Reduction Level

We've set the noise threshold; now it's time to experiment with the Reduction setting. At the moment, however, we have only noise selected in the audio file, and that's not very helpful for adjusting the Reduction setting, because it's the sound of the characters' voices that is important in this file. Let's select the entire audio file so we can see how our settings are affecting the characters' voices as we choose a noise reduction setting.

1   Click the file to ensure it is selected, instead of the Reduce Noise window.

2   As the file plays, press Command-A to select the entire file.

Listen as the character speaks. Notice that speaker's voice now exhibits some degree of tinniness and sounds a bit like a poorly compressed MP3 file downloaded from the Internet.

3   In the Reduce Noise dialog, adjust the Reduction slider until the character's voice begins to sound normal.

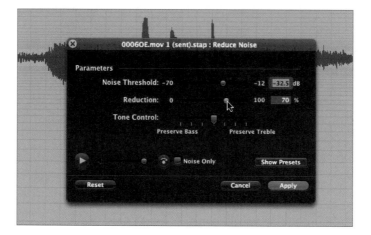

At a setting of around 70 to 75, the tone of the character's voice begins to sound normal while the noise still remains far enough in the background. But let your ears be the judge and continue experimenting with this setting while using the Bypass button to determine how your settings affect the sound.

NOTE ▶ The Tone Control setting is used to apply more emphasis to certain frequency ranges in the audio file. For example, removing noise from the sound of a train rolling by might require a setting more biased toward preserving the bass, whereas removing noise from the sound of birds chirping in a forest might require a setting more biased toward preserving the treble. For human voices, a setting right in the middle is usually OK (unless your character sounds like Barry White, but that's up to your ears to decide).

Applying Noise Reduction

After your experimentation, you should have some pretty good settings for your noise reduction, so you'll now apply these settings to the file and see how they *really* sound. Remember: Every edit you perform is nondestructive, so you can always finesse the settings later.

1 Click the Pause button to stop playback.

2 At the lower right of the Reduce Noise dialog, click the Apply button.

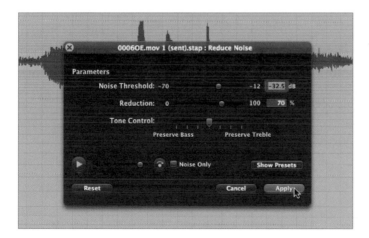

Soundtrack Pro applies your settings to the file and animates the waveform to reflect the changes. You will immediately notice that the noisy parts of the waveform have a much lower amplitude than they did before, showing that the volume of the noise has been reduced. For example, in the following figure, the top image is the audio file before noise reduction, and the bottom image is the audio file after noise reduction. Visually, the difference is striking, but of course, the proof is in the way the file sounds. At the end of the day, you and your ears must be the judge of that.

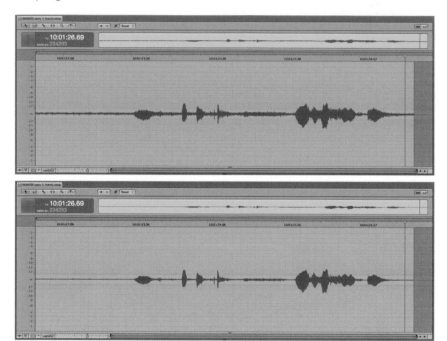

Refining the Noise Reduction Settings

If you listen to your file a few times and decide that the noise reduction settings are not correct, by all means open the Reduce Noise dialog and refine your settings. Here's how to do it.

1   On the Actions tab in the left pane of the workspace, double-click the Reduce Noise action.

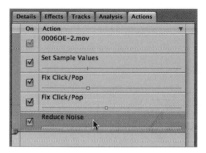

The Reduce Noise dialog reopens.

2   Adjust the noise reduction settings until you've achieved the desired effect. Then click the Apply button.

The new noise reduction settings replace the previous settings.

Rippling Your Changes to Final Cut Pro

You've now removed some pops and clicks and have reduced the noise in the audio file, so it's time to save the file and see how it sounds when played in Final Cut Pro.

1   From the File menu, choose Save, or press Command-S.

A dialog pops up to ask you if you'd like to reference the source audio or save the source audio in your new file

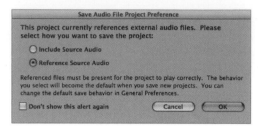

2   Choose Reference Source Audio, and click OK.

Selecting this option creates smaller files that take up less of your hard disk because Soundtrack Pro now references the original audio files, instead of copying the original audio files into your newly saved file. However, if you plan to move the audio file to a new computer, you should include the source audio files to ensure that all the media you need to play the file actually travels with it.

Soundtrack Pro saves the actions in the file.

3   Switch back to Final Cut Pro (either from the Dock, or by pressing Command-Tab until Final Cut Pro is highlighted).

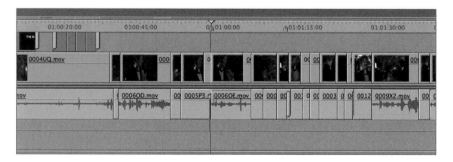

Notice that clip **00060E.mov** now has a green line across the top. This green line indicates that the clip has had a process applied to it.

4   Play the sequence, paying particular attention to the sound of clip **00060E.mov**.

As you can hear, the changes you made in Soundtrack Pro have updated the clip in Final Cut Pro.

Using Soundtrack Pro Scripts to Speed Up Your Work

At this point, you have one great-sounding clip in your Final Cut Pro sequence, but you still have several others to work through. You could open the clips one at a time in Soundtrack Pro and repair them, but that would be very time consuming. Fortunately, there's a quicker way to do the job.

Most video scenes contain audio from only one or two cameras, and because of this, the recording environment is fairly stable and constant. The noise or other problems in the various clips will also be more or less uniform. In the present sequence, for example, clip **00060D.mov** is from the same camera as clip **00060E.mov**. Thus, you should be able to apply the same noise reduction settings to both clips. Here's a trick to speed up this process.

1   In the Final Cut Pro sequence, play and compare clips **00060D.mov** and **00060E.mov**.

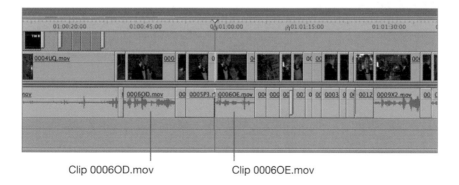

Clip 00060D.mov   Clip 00060E.mov

These clips use the same camera angle, and they sound as though they have the same type of noise in them. Great—that makes things easy.

2   Return to Soundtrack Pro (click the application icon in the Dock).

3   On the Actions tab in the left pane of the workspace, deselect the Set Sample Values action and the two Fix Click/Pop actions.

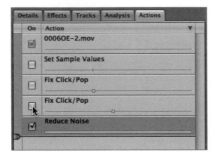

These actions are applicable only to the **0006OE.mov** clip, so you don't want to apply them to any other clips. At the moment, only the Reduce Noise action should be enabled.

4   From Soundtrack Pro's File menu, choose Save As AppleScript.

A Save dialog drops down from the title bar.

5   In the Save As field, type *myNoiseReducer*.

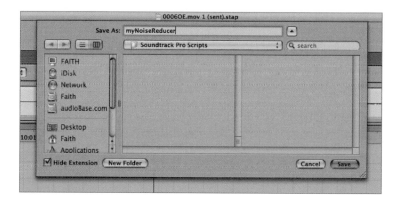

6   Click the Save button.

Soundtrack Pro saves the actions as an AppleScript script. By the way, if you ever need to find this script later, it is located in [your User folder] > Library > Scripts > Soundtrack Pro Scripts folder.

7   Return to Final Cut Pro.

8   Control-click the **0006OD.mov** clip.

9 From the shortcut menu that appears, choose Send To > Soundtrack Pro Script > myNoiseReducer.

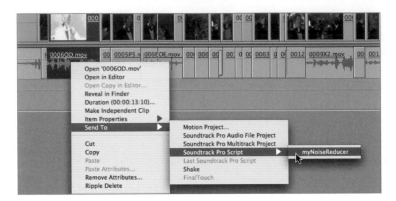

A warning appears asking if you want to convert the selected clip to a Soundtrack Pro project before sending it to the script. If you don't convert the clip to a Soundtrack Pro project, the changes will be applied *destructively*, meaning that the clip will be permanently altered. You don't want that to happen, so the choice you should make here is obvious.

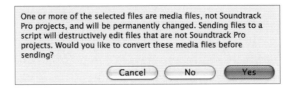

10 Click the Yes button.

A dialog appears asking you to choose a project destination. By default, the last folder you used is selected. This folder happens to be the Soundtrack Files folder you created earlier in this lesson, and that's a great folder to use.

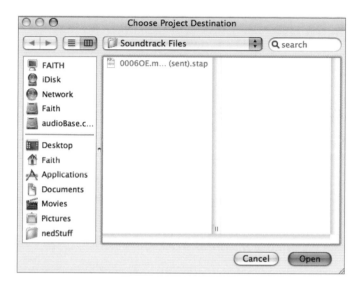

11 Click the Open button.

At this point, the script runs, and several things happen in quick succession. First, the clip opens in Soundtrack Pro. Next, the Reduce Noise action is applied. Then Soundtrack Pro saves the clip. The result of all these actions is that noise reduction is applied to the clip in Final Cut Pro. If you look at the clip in Final Cut Pro, you'll see that a green line appears at the top of clip **0006OD.mov**, indicating filters or processes have been applied to the file. It will play in real time but needs rendering before output.

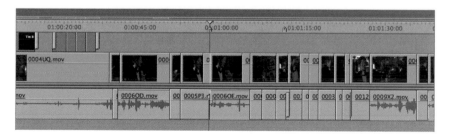

12 Play clip **0006OD.mov** in Final Cut Pro.

Notice that the noise is reduced.

Lesson Review

1. Does the waveform display show an audio file's amplitude, or its frequency spectrum?

2. What is the function of the Sample Edit (Pencil) tool?

3. Is Soundtrack Pro a destructive or a nondestructive audio editor?

4. What kind of common audio problems will Soundtrack Pro analyze in an audio file?

5. Which menu contains options that can be applied to clips as actions?

6. When setting a noise print, which part of the file should you select?

7. What is the best level to use as the Noise Reduce dialog's noise threshold when you begin the process of reducing noise from a file?

8. True or false: Once you apply noise reduction to a file, you cannot undo it.

9. What happens when you save an audio file with actions applied and then return to a Final Cut Pro sequence that contains that audio file?

10. What is the fastest way to apply noise reduction to a set of clips in Final Cut Pro?

Answers

1. Amplitude.

2. The Sample Edit tool lets you change the amplitude of individual samples in an audio file.

3. Soundtrack Pro is a nondestructive audio editor.

4. Soundtrack Pro can analyze an audio file to remove several common problems, including pops and clicks, power-line hum (also called ground-loop hum), DC offset, phase problems, and clipped signals.

5. The Process menu.

6. Select a part of the file that contains *only* noise, and not important parts of the file you want listeners to hear.

7. Set the Noise Threshold slider to the peak level (in dB) of the noise in the file.

8. False.

9. The actions you applied to the file ripple onto your Final Cut Pro sequence, and you now hear the file with the actions applied.

10. Save the actions as an AppleScript script in Soundtrack Pro; then send the Final Cut Pro audio clips to this new Soundtrack Pro AppleScript script to apply the actions.

Keyboard Shortcut

Shift-Z	Fits an entire waveform into the waveform display

3

Lesson **3**

Working with the Frequency Spectrum

In the preceding lesson, you learned how to use the File Editor's Waveform view to edit the amplitude of audio files in many interesting ways. For example, you learned how to remove pops and clicks from an audio file by reducing their volume to a point where they no longer create dramatic volume spikes that cause the playback system's speakers to pop, and you also learned how to decrease the volume of noise in the signal relative to the focus sounds such as dialogue. These are important arrows in the quiver of any audio engineer, and the Waveform view provides valuable visual information to help you in this process.

But audio is more than just amplitude; audio also includes frequency, which is perceived as the sound you hear. The Waveform view says nothing at all about the frequency of the audio files. For that information, you need Soundtrack Pro's Frequency Spectrum view. And by the way, if you are coming to Soundtrack Pro from a DAW such as Digidesign Pro Tools, get ready to be blown away, because the Frequency Spectrum view is unlike anything you've ever seen before. So sit down and strap yourself in. You're about to ride an amazing aural wave.

Using the Frequency Spectrum View

Soundtrack Pro's Frequency Spectrum view is a powerful editing tool because it lets you look at frequencies as they change over time. Most other DAWs will happily show you the waveform of an audio file, but when it comes to the actual sound of the file, you're left to rely on your ears and nothing else. With Soundtrack Pro, however, the process of audio editing is becoming just as visual as it is sonic, and that's great news for people used to using their eyes (like us video editors). Get a visual on this process now by checking out the Frequency Spectrum view.

1   In Soundtrack Pro, open the audio file titled **03 Begin.stap,** or continue working on the audio file you had open at the end of Lesson 2.

2   In the upper-right corner of the File Editor project view, click the Frequency Spectrum View button.

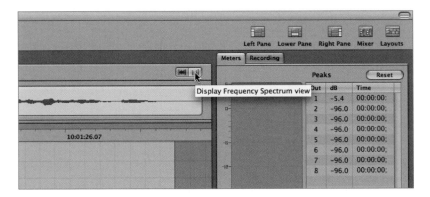

The Waveform view changes to the Frequency Spectrum view. If this is the first time you've seen this view, your initial impression is probably "Wow!" followed immediately by "What does it all mean?" Move on to the next section to see.

NOTE ▸ Logic Pro users can use Soundtrack Pro's Frequency Spectrum View to correct musical problems ranging from a guitar's fret buzz to sibilant vocal tracks. See Lesson 2 to learn how to bring your audio recordings from Logic into Soundtrack.

Exploring the Frequency Spectrum View

At its heart, the Frequency Spectrum view is a three-dimensional graph that displays time along the X axis and frequency along the Y axis. The graph itself is made up of thousands of little dots: one dot for each frequency at each point in time during the duration displayed in the window.

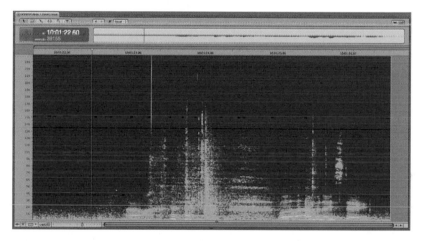

The Frequency Spectrum view

At first glance, you probably noticed the colors displayed in the Frequency Spectrum view. These colors make up the Z axis in this three-dimensional graph, and they represent the amplitudes, or volumes, of the frequencies in the spectrum. In Soundtrack Pro's default Frequency Spectrum view configuration, deep blue means zero amplitude (silence), and bright red means full amplitude (0 dB). Shades of yellow, green, and blue represent the varying levels of volume for each of the frequencies represented.

As you can imagine, this view is incredibly powerful, and it allows you to visualize audio in ways never before possible. For example, have you ever wondered what noise looks like? Well, no need to imagine any longer, because you can get a graphical representation of noise by following the first step in the next exercise.

1   On the Actions tab in the left pane of the workspace, deselect the Reduce Noise action.

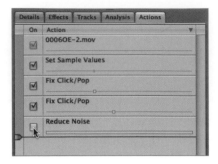

The Frequency Spectrum view updates to display the noise you removed from this file in the preceding lesson. The difference is dramatic. As you can see, the noise looks like random dots of frequency spread across the audio file, in much the same way as noise in a video signal looks like random dots of colors spread across the video frame. In either situation, the result is quite ugly, so let's get that noise back out of this audio file.

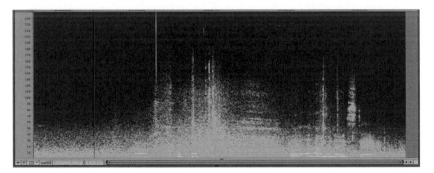

2   On the Actions tab, select the Reduce Noise action again.

The noise is once again removed from the audio file.

Linear Versus Logarithmic Frequency Scales

The human ear is a funny tool, and it works in ways you would not immediately expect. In fact, we tend to hear frequencies as ratios, rather than as a direct linear expression of the sounds emitted by the world around us. In terms of pitch, doubling a frequency (a frequency ratio of 2) is perceived as an increase of one octave. For example, the space between 60 Hz and 120 Hz represents a full octave. Similarly, the space between 500 Hz and 1000 Hz represents a full octave. And the space between 10,000 Hz and 20,000 Hz also represents just a single octave—unbelievable, but true!

For this reason, most frequency scales in the music world are represented logarithmically instead of linearly. The logarithmic frequency scale more naturally mimics the way we hear and think about sound. Indeed, most of the sounds we hear inhabit a frequency range of 10,000 Hz (10 kHz) or below. We actually hear very little of the frequency range above 16,000 Hz (16 kHz), and basically nothing above 24,000 Hz (24 kHz), which conveniently is the full frequency range of the 48 kHz audio files commonly used in digital video today. (Notice that the maximum range of our hearing, at 24 kHz, is exactly half the 48 kHz sampling rate used in audio files for digital video—it isn't a coincidence.)

Without going too much deeper into the science of sound, suffice it to say that the most intuitive way for humans to look at sound is on the logarithmic scale. This is why all the plug-ins in Soundtrack Pro, such as the Channel EQ plug-in shown in the window here, use the logarithmic scale to display frequencies.

NOTE ▶ The Channel EQ plug-in uses the logarithmic frequency scale to represent sound. Notice that the scale is dominated by frequencies below 1 kHz, and that this scale devotes barely any space to frequencies above 10,000 Hz (10 kHz). The vertical lines in the Channel EQ display roughly correspond to the octave settings we can hear, which means this Channel EQ display shows approximately nine octaves of sound.

By default, Soundtrack Pro's Frequency Spectrum view shows the linear frequency scale. As you'll see a bit later in this lesson, the linear frequency scale is great for analyzing and cleaning up an audio file, but it is not the most intuitive or musical way to look at the frequency range. Take a moment now to explore the difference between the linear and logarithmic frequency scales.

1   At the left edge of the File Editor project view, Control-click the scale.

A shortcut menu appears. As you can see, the linear frequency scale is currently displayed.

2   From the shortcut menu, choose Logarithmic.

The File Editor updates to display the frequency spectrum logarithmically.

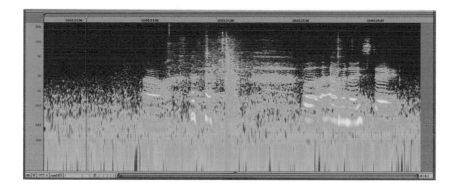

Beautiful—isn't that much more representative of the way you see sound? Well, beauty is in the eye (and also the ear) of the beholder. It's up to you to decide which view you prefer, but while you experiment, keep this in mind: If you want to look at sound musically, use the logarithmic display; if you want to look at sound analytically, try the linear display.

Controlling the Spectrum

No doubt about it: The spectrum display is pretty psychedelic. But what you see now is not all it has to show. In fact, you can adjust the display of the Frequency Spectrum view in many interesting ways. This view's greatest asset is its capability to let you literally *see* the sound you are working with and visually understand how the frequencies in the file work together to make the sound you hear. You may find it easier to see the sound by adjusting the spectrum controls, so try that now.

1   In the spectrum display, Control-click the background.

2   In the shortcut menu that appears, choose Show Spectrum Controls.

The Spectrum View HUD (heads-up display) opens. Some of its settings you've seen already, but others may be new and confusing, so take the next moments to explore the most important settings in this window.

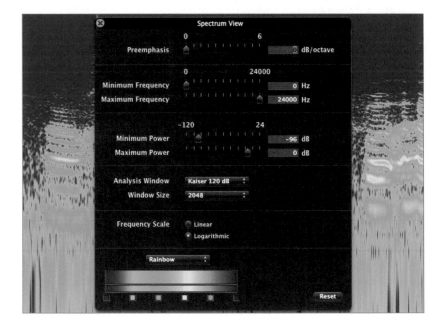

Setting the Frequency Range

The Spectrum View HUD's frequency controls let you zoom in on certain frequencies and make them fill the spectrum display. As you edit your audio, for example, you may want to focus on the vocals and ignore the other sounds in the audio file. Vocals mainly inhabit a frequency range of 500 Hz to 2500 Hz. You'll now limit the Frequency Spectrum view to display only this frequency range.

1 In the Spectrum View HUD, set the Minimum Frequency slider to approximately *500* Hz.

NOTE ▶ This isn't rocket science, so a close approximation is probably good enough, but if you really want to get exact, you can always type a Hz setting in the field to the right of the slider.

2 In the Spectrum View HUD, set the Maximum Frequency slider to approximately *2500* Hz.

A quick check of the scale along the left of the File Editor project view shows that the spectrum display now shows only frequencies between 500 Hz and 2500 Hz.

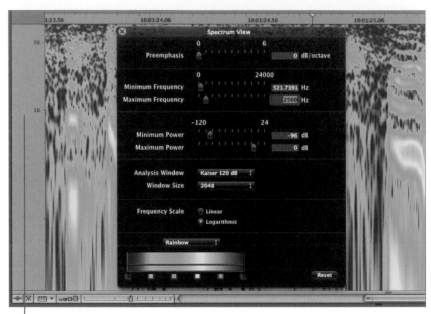

Scale

Adjusting the Spectrum Power Controls

The Spectrum View HUD's power controls are sort of like contrast settings. These controls are primarily used to limit the Frequency Spectrum view's display to certain decibel ranges. For example, all of the vocals in this audio file are above −60 dB, and most of the background noise is not. You can adjust the power to exclude from view all of the background noise so you can focus solely on the vocals.

1   In the Spectrum View HUD, set the Minimum Power slider to approximately –60 dB.

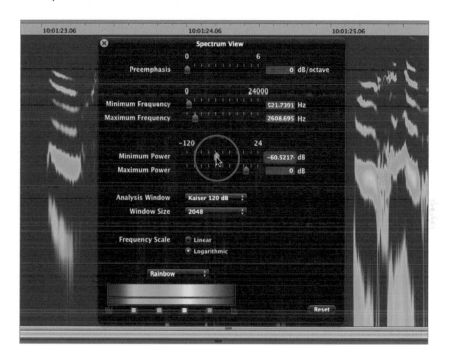

Any frequency below –60 dB drops out of the display. But now there's a new problem. Limiting the minimum power of the view to –60 dB makes it difficult to see which of the remaining frequencies have more power, or a stronger amplitude, because everything looks green. You'll change that now.

2   In the Spectrum View HUD, set the Maximum Power slider to approximately –25 dB (or until some red starts creeping into the view).

So after all these settings, you are now looking at frequencies between 500 Hz and 2500 Hz that are louder than –60 dB but quieter than –25 dB. You've pretty well isolated the vocals in this audio file.

3   Play the file.

All that's left visible in the spectrum display is the talking.

Adjusting View Colors

Right now you are looking at the spectrum in rainbow colors. Loud frequencies are red, quiet frequencies are blue, and the remaining frequencies span a rainbow of colors in between. If this doesn't appeal to you, you can change the colors of the display to mimic vintage audio gear or to appear red hot. In fact, you can tailor this display in several ways. Sometimes playing with these settings lets you see things in the frequencies you may have missed using one of the other configurations.

1 From the Color pop-up menu at the bottom of the Spectrum View HUD, choose Red Hot.

The Frequency Spectrum view updates to show you fire and brimstone. OK, that's a bit melodramatic, but the Frequency Spectrum view is indeed now displaying a very red view of your audio. More to the point, that very noisy and hard-to-look-at audio file that you started with now shows some useful information in a way that is clean and easy to understand, and you can see exactly where the vocals sit in this audio file.

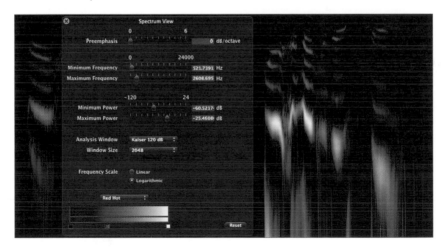

Resetting the Frequency Spectrum View

You've tweaked the Frequency Spectrum view to display only the audio file's vocals, in red. That's great if you're just editing vocals, but you have some more important audio restoration work to do, so reset the Frequency Spectrum view before you continue.

1   At the bottom right of the Spectrum View HUD, click the Reset button.

The Frequency Spectrum view is reset to its default settings.

2   At the top left of the Spectrum View HUD, click the close button.

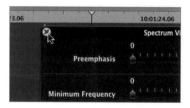

The Spectrum View HUD closes.

Working with Frequency

Now that you know the basics of how to modify the Frequency Spectrum view to isolate frequencies and ensure that only useful information appears on the screen, you'll look a bit deeper and see how you can use this view to restore some audio from the **Blind Date** sequence.

If you listen closely to the audio in the **Blind Date** sequence, you can tell that the audio was captured from the individual camera microphones—it's immediately apparent because every camera angle has a slightly different sound to it. From some of the camera angles, there are extra bits of noise you need to remove. For example, clip **0003A2.mov** has a high-pitched hum that is disconcerting to listen to, and it's particularly noticeable because the clips before and after it do not have a similar noise. As the audio technician, you have the responsibility to remove that extraneous sound.

1   Switch back to the Final Cut Pro sequence you had open in the preceding lesson, or open Lesson 03 > **03 Begin.fcp**.

2   In the Current Timecode field at the upper left of the Timeline, type *01:01:11:11* and press Return.

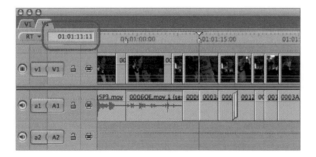

The playhead jumps to the beginning of clip **0003A2.mov** (note that this is not clip **0003A2.mov 1**, which comes later in the sequence).

3   Play clip **0003A2.mov** and listen closely.

Notice the soft but audible hum across the entire clip.

4   Send the clip to Soundtrack Pro as an audio file project (for more information, see the section "Opening Audio Files from Final Cut Pro" in Lesson 2).

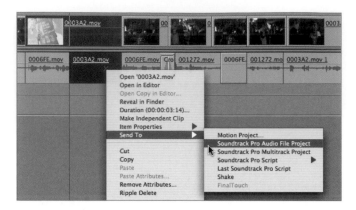

The clip opens in Soundtrack Pro's Waveform view. You need to look at this clip in the Frequency Spectrum view, so you need to switch views.

5 At the upper right of the File Editor project view, click the Display Frequency Spectrum button.

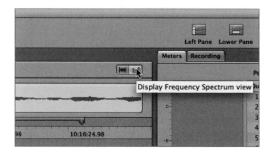

The audio file is now displayed in the Frequency Spectrum view.

Adding Digital Signal Processing Effects

With the clip now open in the Frequency Spectrum view, you can see exactly where that high-pitched hum is coming from. Indeed, there are several green horizontal lines of frequency clearly visible in the Frequency Spectrum view. All of these horizontal lines of frequency add nothing to the sound of the scene and should be removed (for viewers, few things distract attention from a scene more than steady hums like these).

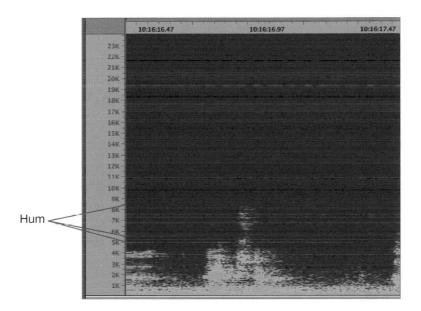

But is that all the hum there is in the file? Maybe not. You can use a trick to accentuate the softer frequencies and check visually to see whether there are hums you may be missing. For this check, you'll apply a dynamic range compressor.

In audio terms, *dynamic range* refers to the difference between the softest and the loudest sounds in a file. When you compress the dynamic range of a file, you decrease the difference between the softest and loudest sounds. In other words, you make the softest sounds louder, and the loudest sounds softer, which leads to a leveling out of the sound. Let's add a dynamic range compressor and look at the effect.

1 Play the clip and get a good feel for the way it sounds.

2 From the main menu bar, choose Process > Effects > Dynamics > Compressor.

NOTE ▶ All of Soundtrack Pro's DSP (digital signal processing) effects are available from the Process menu as actions. You can apply these effects to any audio file nondestructively and reorder them as you please.

The Compressor dialog opens.

Using Plug-In Presets

A compressor is a fairly complex DSP plug-in, and it takes practice to understand how a compressor really works. You'll learn more about the theory later.

For now, you'll use one of the Soundtrack Pro compressor's built-in vocal presets.

> **NOTE ▶** For detailed information on how to use a compressor (and several other important audio mastering plug-ins that come with Soundtrack Pro), visit macProVideo.com and check out the tutorial "Logic 202: Plug-ins, Unplugged." Logic uses the same plug-ins as Soundtrack Pro, so you'll find lots of good information you can use to make your videos sound punchy and professional.

1 At the bottom right of the Compressor dialog, click the Show Presets button.

The Presets drawer opens.

2 In the Presets drawer, click the disclosure triangles to display the User Presets and then the 04 Voice presets.

3 Select the Vocal Compressor 01 preset.

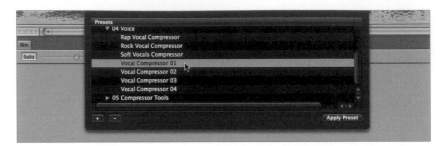

4 Click the Apply Preset button.

The compressor controls update to reflect the preset's settings. Even more noticeable, the file's volume increases. However, the compressor has not yet been applied to the file, so the file still looks the same in the Frequency Spectrum view. You'll change that now.

5 At the right side of the Compressor dialog, click the flashing Apply button.

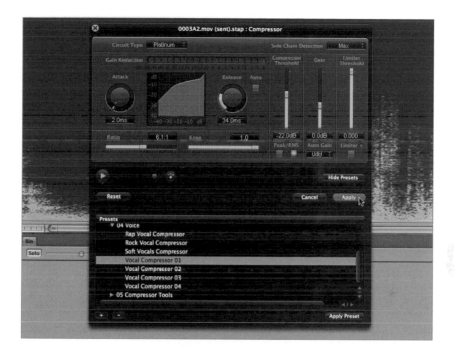

The compressor is applied to the audio file, and some noticeable changes occur in the file's appearance in the spectrum display. For starters, the file looks much louder, as all the frequencies are more pronounced. You can see much more noise in the file than was previously visible, but even more important, you can now see some additional horizontal lines of hum around 16 kHz and 17 kHz that were not visible before. These need to be removed from the file.

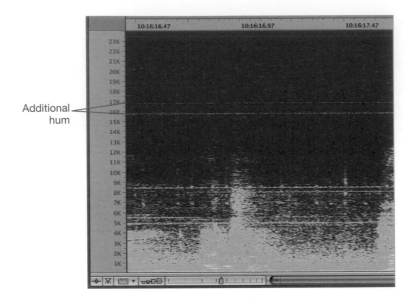

Additional hum

6 Stop playback.

Removing Frequencies

The capability to edit and remove specific frequencies from an audio file is one of the major advantages that Soundtrack Pro offers compared to other common audio postproduction tools on the market. Using the Frequency Selection tool, you can easily select and delete frequencies you don't want in your file. This tool is particularly handy for deleting solid hums like the ones plaguing this clip.

1 From the waveform editing tools, choose the Frequency Selection tool (or press W).

The Frequency Selection tool works just like any other selection tool you've used: Just drag to select the frequencies you want.

2   In the spectrum display, drag a selection rectangle around the horizontal line at 17 kHz from the beginning of the file until the end.

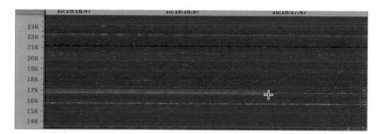

3   Press Delete.

The selected frequency is deleted.

4   Select and delete the remaining horizontal lines of frequency in the file.

NOTE ▸ To help you select frequencies, you may want to zoom in closer on the frequency ranges you are editing. Remember: You can Control-click in the spectrum display and choose Show Spectrum Controls to open the Spectrum View HUD. Use the Spectrum View HUD's Minimum Frequency and Maximum Frequency sliders to zoom in on the frequencies before selecting them. For more information, see the section "Setting the Frequency Range" earlier in this lesson.

When you are finished editing the file, it should look similar to the following figure. Admittedly, you've removed thin swaths of frequency, and this could result in a comb filter effect (a series of regularly spaced spikes) on the file; however, a small comb filter effect is much better than a constant hum. Also, most of the power in the vocal range is between 500 and 2500 Hz. You've removed only frequencies above 5000 Hz, so this edit will have little effect on the sound of the vocals.

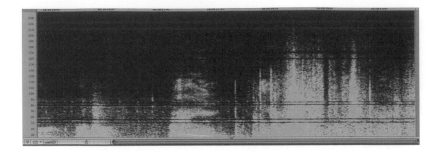

5   Play the file.

The hum is gone. The file still includes lots of noise, but you now know how to remove that. To practice your new skills, try creating a noise print and reducing the remaining noise (a good place to pull a noise print is directly after the director says "Action!").

NOTE ▶ Before removing noise, it's often helpful to remove any extraneous sounds such as the hum in the file discussed here. This approach enables you to focus the noise print on the noise itself, without worrying about the hum.

Finishing Up

Now that the file is cleaned, get rid of the compressor action so that the clip remains at the same volume as the other clips in the **Blind Date** sequence; then save the file.

1   From the Actions list, select the Compressor action.

2   Press Delete.

The Compressor action is deleted.

3   Save your audio file (for more information on saving audio files that have actions attached, see the section "Rippling Your Changes to Final Cut Pro" in Lesson 2).

> **NOTE** ▶ You can be fairly certain that any of the **Blind Date** sequence clips shot on the same camera as this clip will have the same hum in them. Consequently, you can safely save this action set as an AppleScript script and apply it to any of the Final Cut Pro sequence clips that use this camera angle. For more information, see the section "Using Soundtrack Pro Scripts to Speed Up Your Work" in Lesson 2.

Lesson Review

1.   Which frequency scale most closely matches the way humans perceive sound: the linear or logarithmic scale?

2.   What does the Spectrum View HUD do?

3.   True or false: You cannot zoom in on frequencies in the Frequency Spectrum view.

4.   What does a dynamic range compressor do?

5.   How do you delete specific frequencies from a file?

Answers

1.   The logarithmic scale.

2.   The Spectrum View HUD lets you control the way the Frequency Spectrum view displays frequencies.

3.   False. You can use the Spectrum View HUD's Minimum Frequency and Maximum Frequency settings to zoom in on specific frequencies.

4.   A dynamic range compressor makes the softest sounds in an audio file louder and the loudest sounds softer, which leads to a leveling out of the file's sound.

5.   Use the Frequency Selection tool to select the frequencies and then press Delete.

4

Lesson **4**

Recording in Soundtrack Pro

So far we've spent a lot of time exploring Soundtrack Pro features you can use to clean up and repair audio from your Final Cut Pro projects. Specifically, we've looked at ways to make dialogue sound better, and for good reason: In most videos, dialogue is the center of the viewer's attention. People want to see and hear what the onscreen characters are saying; in fact, dialogue is so important to the perceived quality of the final project that even the tone or accent used by a character can make or break a scene. Because of the importance of dialogue, an entire audio postproduction industry has sprung up to address dialogue replacement. Happily for Final Cut Studio owners, Soundtrack Pro is an incredible dialogue-replacement tool.

In this lesson, you'll learn how to record your own dialogue to replace some of the dialogue in the **Blind Date** project. Along the way, you'll learn important recording techniques that will take you far beyond recording dialogue. In fact, Soundtrack Pro is an advanced audio recording and tracking program with well-developed mixing tools, so you can even use multiple microphones and inputs to record multiple voiceover actors (or instruments) at the same time.

Opening a Multitrack Project

By now you are familiar with techniques for opening single audio files in
Soundtrack Pro, but what if you want to edit the audio from an entire sequence
in one shot? For example, you might want to apply the same compression
settings to all the clips in a specific track, not just to individual clips. In Final
Cut Pro, you can't assign effects to an entire track in a sequence, but in
Soundtrack Pro, you can. Let's open a multitrack project from Final Cut Pro
and begin exploring the process.

1   In Final Cut Pro, open the project **04 Begin.fcp**, or continue working on
    the Final Cut Pro project you had open at the end of Lesson 3.

2   In Final Cut Pro's bin, ensure that the **V1** sequence is selected (if this
    sequence is not selected, you won't be able to select the menu item in
    the next step).

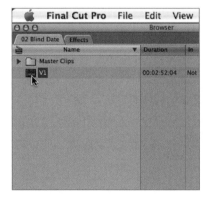

3   Choose File > Send To > Soundtrack Pro Multitrack Project.

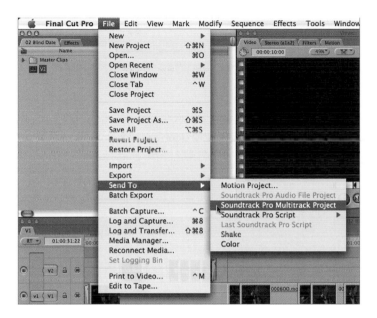

4   In the Save dialog that appears, type *myMultitrackProject.stmp* and then click Save.

The project opens as a multitrack project in Soundtrack Pro.

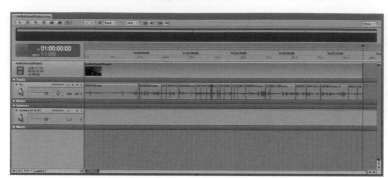

This project includes only one track of audio, but that is about to change. You'll add another track a few steps down the road. But first, let's get a feel for the dialogue you will replace as this lesson progresses.

Using the Timecode HUD

The Timecode heads-up display, or HUD, shows you the playhead's position in the sequence as an SMPTE timecode value. It's also useful for jumping to specific points in the project.

In this lesson, you are going to replace the dialogue spoken by the very agreeable Spanish character that our hero questions when she first walks into the café. Let's jump to the beginning of that scene now, using the Timecode HUD.

1   In Soundtrack Pro, choose Window > HUDs > Timecode.

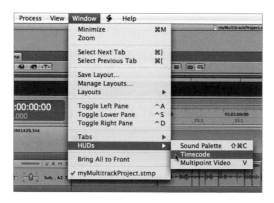

The Timecode HUD opens and floats over the project.

NOTE ▸ Drag the lower-right corner of the Timecode HUD to make the HUD bigger or smaller. Changing the size of the HUD can be handy when you need make it big enough to see the timecode value from across the room (for example, when recording Foley sounds), or when you need to make it small enough to sit in a particular section of the screen.

2 Position the pointer over the seconds value.

Two white arrows appear directly over the seconds value: one at the top and one at the bottom of the Timecode HUD.

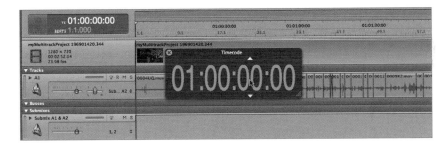

3   Drag up until the seconds display reads *30*.

As you drag, notice that the playhead moves across the Timeline. This is important to note, because the playhead's position always reflects the timecode value displayed in the Timecode HUD.

4   Play the project (and watch the scene) to approximately timecode value 01:01:00:00.

In this section of the scene, the Spanish character says "yes" several times. You will record new dialogue for these "yeses" later in this chapter, so make sure you have a good feel for the pacing and rhythm of this scene. You may want to play it a few times just to be sure, because in a moment, you are going to be the voice actor! Reset the playhead to the beginning of this scene, using a different technique this time.

5   In the Timecode HUD, double-click the display.

The Timecode HUD updates to display a text field.

6   Type *01:00:30:00* and press Return.

The playhead jumps to exactly 30 seconds and 0 frames into the sequence.

NOTE ▶ To position the playhead, you can also double-click the timecode area in the upper-left corner of the Timeline to open a text field and type a timecode value.

Working with Tracks

Tracks form the base of any project in Soundtrack Pro. In fact, right now you are working on a multitrack project, which means you're working on a project that can have more than one track of audio. With all these tracks available, it helps to know how to create, rearrange, and delete them.

Creating Tracks

The current project has only one track, and this track contains audio you need, so you don't want to record over it. That means you need to create a new track before you can start recording.

1   Choose Multitrack > Add Track (Command-T).

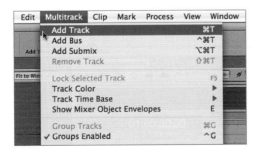

A new track (titled Track 2) is created in the project. You can also create new tracks using a shortcut menu.

2 Control-click anywhere on the header of Track 2.

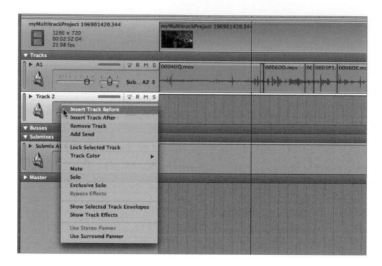

A shortcut menu appears. At the top of this menu are two options: Insert Track Before and Insert Track After. As you might expect, the first option inserts a track before the currently selected track, and the second option inserts a new track after the currently selected track.

3 Choose Insert Track Before.

Track 3 is created before Track 2.

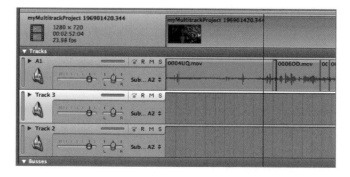

Reordering Tracks

Track 3 now sits before Track 2. That's a bit out of order, so you'll now do some rearranging.

1 Drag Track 3 under Track 2.

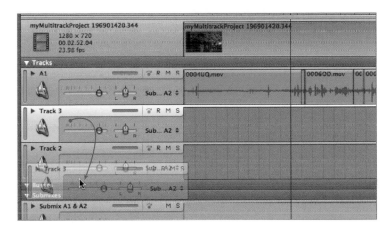

Deleting Tracks

In a few moments, you will be making your first voiceover recording. However, you need only one empty track to record into, so let's get Track 3 out of the way.

1 Control-click Track 3.

2 From the shortcut menu that appears, choose Remove Track (Shift-Command-T).

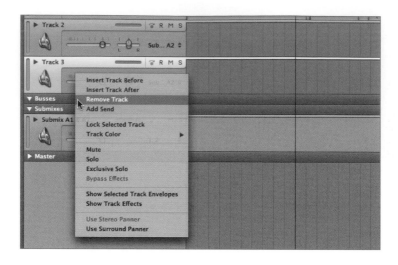

Track 3 is deleted.

Naming Tracks

The empty track is currently named Track 2. That's not a very descriptive name, so let's change it.

1   Click to select the words *Track 2*.

A text field appears.

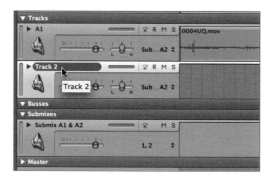

2   Type *myVoiceOver* and press Return.

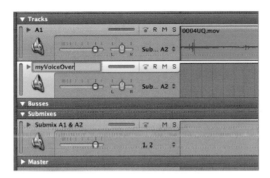

The track is renamed myVoiceOver.

Locking Tracks

To avoid making accidental edits to tracks, it often helps to lock them. This ensures that you don't accidentally move clips or record-enable tracks that you don't want edited. You'll lock the first track in the project to ensure it does not accidentally get changed in any way.

1   Control-click the track titled A1.

2   From the shortcut menu that appears, choose Lock Selected Track.

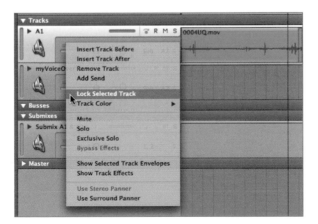

The track is textured with diagonal lines, indicating that it cannot be edited.

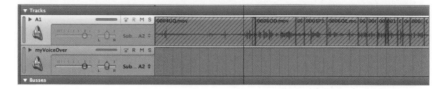

NOTE ▶ To unlock the track, choose Unlock Track from the same short-cut menu.

Setting Up for Recording

At this point, the playhead is positioned at 30 seconds into the project, and you have a new, empty track ready to record into. It's almost time to do some recording. However, you need to do a bit of setup before you get to the big recording moment. First you must ensure that the correct audio interface input is selected and that you are recording the correct number of audio channels.

Setting Controls in the Recording Tab

When it comes to recording in Soundtrack Pro, the Recording tab is where all the heavy lifting is done. This tab contains level meters you can use to monitor the input source, as well as settings to configure the number of channels you will record in each track. The Recording tab is located in the right pane, so follow the steps here to ensure that the tab is visible.

1   In the upper-right corner of the Toolbar, click the Right Pane button, or choose Window > Toggle Right Pane (Control-D).

The right pane appears.

2   Click the Recording tab.

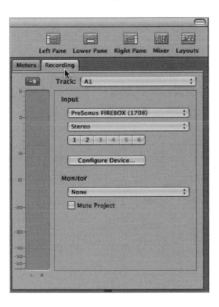

Choosing a Track to Record

Soundtrack Pro is an extremely versatile multitrack recording utility. In fact, you can record multiple tracks at once and even assign different input, channel, and monitor settings for each track (we'll explore these features in a moment).

Because of the high level of configurability, you must be very sure you've selected the correct track in the Recording tab before you start configuring the track for recording.

1   From the Track menu at the top of the Recording tab, choose the myVoiceOver track.

Choosing a Recording Input

Each track you record to can be assigned a different input in Soundtrack Pro. This feature can be very handy if you are recording using multiple microphones connected to multiple audio interfaces on your system. The recording you are about to do is not as complex as that, but you still need to tell Soundtrack Pro what audio interface you will use.

If you don't have an audio interface attached to your computer, the built-in microphone or the default inputs are all that will be available. If you have an Apple laptop or iMac, you can complete this lesson using only the microphone contained in your computer. Mac Pro or PowerMac users, however, will need to have an audio interface and a microphone to continue, because there is no microphone included with those systems directly out of the box.

1   From the Recording tab's Input menu, choose your audio interface or microphone input.

Note that initially Soundtrack Pro is set to use your default audio interface, as assigned by your system's Audio/Midi Setup utility. However, you can visit Soundtrack Pro's preferences to set a specific default input. You can also set the default channel, monitor, and latency compensation in the Recording pane of Soundtrack Pro preferences.

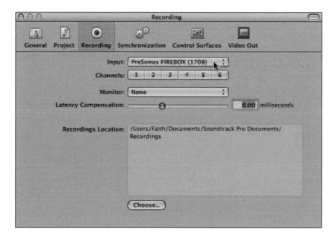

Choosing a Channel Configuration

The channel configuration determines how many channels of audio you will record to each track. You can choose one channel (mono), two channels (stereo) or any combination of channels all the way up to six channels (5.1 surround). Unlike most other DAWs, which record each channel as a separate track in the Timeline, Soundtrack Pro records all channels on a single clip. As you'll discover in Appendix A, "Surround Mixing," recording all the channels in one clip makes it extremely easy to edit and mix multichannel projects. For now, however, you are recording through a single microphone only, and a single microphone has just one channel. You need to set Soundtrack Pro up accordingly.

1   In the Recording tab, click the Input Channel pop-up menu.

2   Choose Mono.

You will now record one channel of audio only.

Adjusting the Channel Setting

If your audio interface has more than one input, you can connect your microphone to any input on the audio interface—the choice is yours. However, you still need to tell Soundtrack Pro what input you are using, or it will try to record from input 1. You do this by setting the channel buttons.

At the moment, only one channel button is active, because you are about to record a mono file. If you are recording through channel 1 of your audio interface, no more work needs to be done. If you are recording through a different channel, follow the steps here.

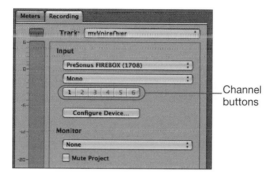

NOTE ▶ If your audio interface lets you name inputs, those names will appear in the Channel Button pop-up menus.

1   Click and hold the first channel button.

A pop-up menu appears.

2   Choose the channel that your microphone is plugged in to.

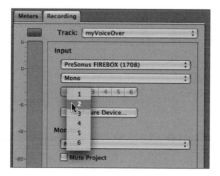

Displaying Recording Settings in the Track Header

If you find that these visits to the Recording tab keep you from concentrating on the action in the Timeline, you can adjust your input settings directly in each track's header. However, you must have the Timeline track height set to medium or large for these settings to appear.

1 At the lower left of the Timeline, set the Timeline track height to medium.

The tracks become taller, and the input settings are now displayed directly in the track header.

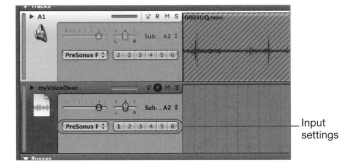

Recording a Single Take

It's time to make your first recording with Soundtrack Pro! But first, a word of advice: If you have some headphones handy, get them out and use them. You can't listen to the project through speakers while recording, because the sound of the project will feed back into the microphone and corrupt your recording. Additionally, it helps to use headphones that have a good ear cup and to play the project back at low volume while recording the voiceover. These precautions help to minimize the "bleed," or the amount of sound that escapes from your headphones and is in turn picked up by the microphone. You don't want any of the sound from the source project in your new recording, and following these few basic precautions can really help to minimize this problem.

Choosing a Recording Destination

By default, Soundtrack Pro saves all of your recordings in your Documents > Soundtrack Pro Documents > Recordings path. If you want to record to a different folder, follow these steps.

1   Choose Soundtrack Pro > Preferences.

2   At the top of the Preferences pane, click the Recording button.

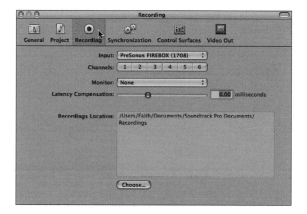

The Recording pane appears. At the bottom of the pane is a Recordings Location area.

3   At the bottom of the Recordings Location area, click the Choose button.

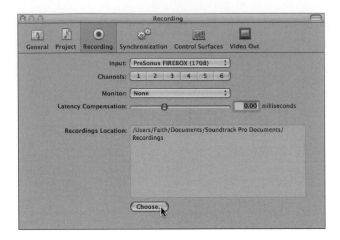

A Finder pane drops down from the top of the Recording pane.

4   Navigate to the folder where you want to save your recordings, and click Open.

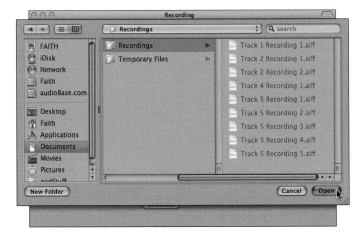

The folder is selected as the destination for your newly recorded files.

5   Close the Preferences pane.

Arming a Track for Recording

The myVoiceOver track you created at the beginning of this chapter is ready to go, so let's arm it for recording now.

When you arm a track for recording, you essentially tell Soundtrack Pro to get ready for the recording that is about to occur. You can't record into a track without first arming it for recording. If you try, Soundtrack Pro will create a new track and place your recording in the new track. Depending on the situation, this may be fine, but for the situation at hand, you want to record directly into the myVoiceOver track you've already created.

1 On the myVoiceOver track, click the R (Arm for Recording) button.

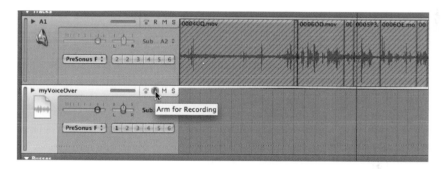

The track turns red, indicating that it is armed for recording.

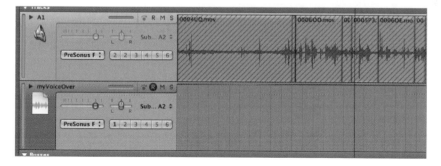

Setting a Recording Level

As soon as you arm a track for recording, the level meter on the Recording tab displays the signal level of the sound coming through your microphone. Before recording, you must adjust the level of the input on your sound card to ensure that you record at the appropriate volume.

In previous lessons, you saw how important it is to minimize the amount of noise in your audio. It doesn't matter how good your recording equipment is; there's always going to be some noise in your signal or the sound you record. The goal is to minimize the level of this noise relative to the level of your recorded sound. This relationship is called the signal-to-noise ratio of your file, and it's always best to have a big difference between the level of noise and the level of your recording. Consequently, you should always record at the highest level you can without clipping the recording (clipping occurs when you record levels above 0 dB on the digital scale).

That's the theory, but in reality any input level that peaks between approximately –6 dB and –3 dB is a good level to use. This leaves you a little bit of headroom (room between your peak recording level and 0 dB) to ensure that you don't clip the recording if, for example, you get a little excited and exclaim a few words more loudly than you did in practice.

1   Locate the input controls on your audio interface.

2   Say the words "Test, test, check, test" repeatedly and watch the Recording tab's input level meter.

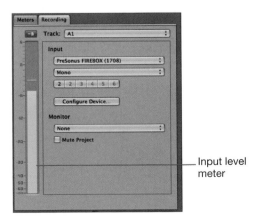

Input level meter

NOTE ▶ The input level meter is a peak-and-hold meter. This means it holds a line at the peaks of the signal level for a few seconds, so you can get a good read on what level your signal is peaking at.

3   Adjust the audio input until your test speech is peaking at approximately −3 dB.

Resetting the Peak Indicator

The peak indicator is the small box just above the input level meter. This indicator shows you the highest audio level incurred since the last time the indicator was reset. Even more important, the peak indicator changes from gray to red the instant any part of your input signal goes above 0 dB, giving you a hard-to-miss visual warning that your recording is going to be clipped.

Peak indicator

1   To reset the peak indicator, click it once.

The indicator sets itself to the current peak in the signal.

▶ ### Setting Monitor Output

If you are using multiple audio interfaces on your system, you may sometimes need to set up headphones or other monitors through an audio interface different from the one you are recording through. The Monitor menu on Soundtrack Pro's Recording tab lets you do this.

However, take note: *You must make sure that your microphone is not near the speakers you set as your monitors.* **This is very important!**

If your microphone is near your monitor speaker, the sound coming out of your speakers will go straight back into the microphone. It will then loop through your system and be sent straight back out the speakers, and again, back into the microphone. Each time this loop feeds back into the microphone, it gets louder. This is called a feedback loop, and it can do serious damage not only to your gear but also to your ears. This is why the Monitor pop-up menu is set to None by default. Unless you have good reason to change this, you should leave this setting untouched.

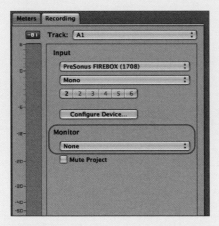

Recording a Take

The playhead is currently parked at 30 seconds into the project, which is the start of the scene containing the Spanish character. In the following steps, you will record yourself saying "yes" before replacing the vocals from the other character. Get your golden voice ready, and don't be scared to give it a bit of attitude. If you're not a man, lower the tone of your voice a bit and pretend.

> **NOTE ▶** You may want to quickly view this scene to remind yourself of the content before returning the playhead to the project's 30-second mark.

If you have headphones, put them on. In any situation, turn off your monitor speakers so you don't get feedback into your recording.

With these precautions in place, you're ready to make a recording.

1   In the transport area at the bottom of the workspace, click the Record button.

The playhead begins passing along the Timeline, and a new red clip is created in the myVoiceOver track. Soundtrack Pro is now recording.

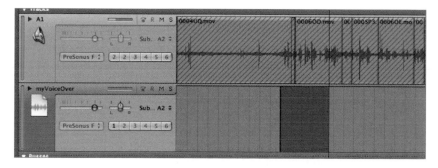

2 Watch the action, and say "yes" wherever the Spanish character says "yes."

3 When the scene is finished, press the spacebar (or click the Record button a second time) to stop recording.

A newly recorded clip is now in your Timeline.

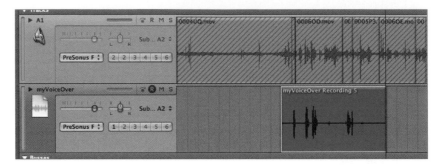

Collecting the Project

When you record a file in Soundtrack Pro, it is automatically saved to the location on your hard disk that you specify in your Soundtrack Pro Recording preferences (see "Choosing a Recording Destination" earlier in this lesson). While this is a great way to ensure all of your recordings are stored in one easy-to-locate folder on your computer, it's not the best approach if you want to archive your project after you finish it, or if you need to move the project between computers while working on it.

This is where *collecting* the project comes in handy. When you save a Soundtrack Pro project as a collected project, Soundtrack Pro automatically gathers all of the audio files used in the project (including recordings) and places them on your computer in a folder of your choice.

But that's not the only handy feature; Soundtrack Pro also places all further recordings directly into the collected project's new folder. In fact, the File menu's Save command even changes to Save Collected, as you'll see in the steps that follow. If you want to keep all your recordings tightly gathered in a single folder for each project you are working on, it's often a good idea to save a collected version of your project directly after making your first recording,

1   From Soundtrack Pro's menu bar, choose File > Save As.

The Save As dialog appears. At the bottom of the dialog are some options unique to Soundtrack Pro. Specifically, there is a Collect Audio Files checkbox.

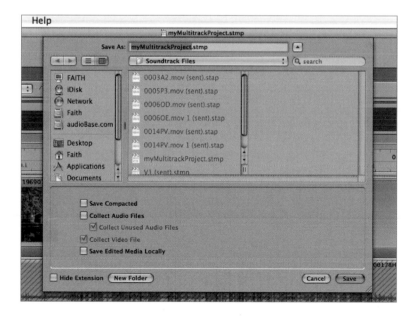

2   On the Save As dialog, click the Collect Audio Files checkbox to select it.

Selecting this checkbox tells Soundtrack Pro to gather all the audio files used for the project and place them with the saved project file. However, you do have some decisions to make.

▶   **Collect Unused Audio Files**—Keep this checkbox selected if you want Soundtrack Pro to include audio files that you have not used in the project itself. For example, you may have recordings, loops, or music files you were testing that you want to include with the saved file, just in case you decide to use them later.

▶   **Collect Video File**—Keep this checkbox selected if you want to include the video file used in the project. Remember that this file may take up a large amount of space on your hard disk. If, for example, you intend to collect the project and archive it to DVD, collecting the video may make the project far too big for the disc.

3   Deselect the Collect Unused Audio Files and Collect Video File checkboxes.

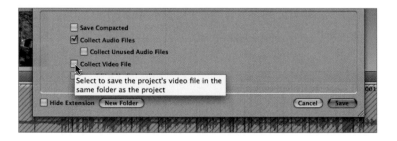

Because several audio files will now be gathered and placed in a folder (called Media) in the same location as the project file, you may find it handy to create a new folder to hold the collected project. You'll do that now.

4   Navigate to the place where you want to save the collected project (the steps here save the project on the desktop, which makes it easy to locate and delete after you are finished with these lessons).

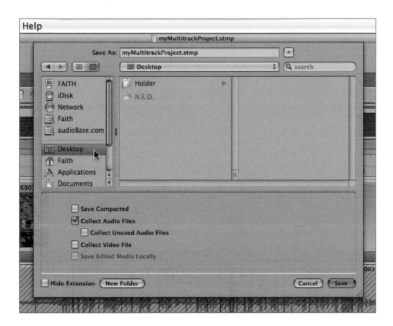

5   At the bottom of the Save As dialog, click the New Folder button.

6   In the New Folder dialog that appears, type *myCollectedProject* and click
the Create button.

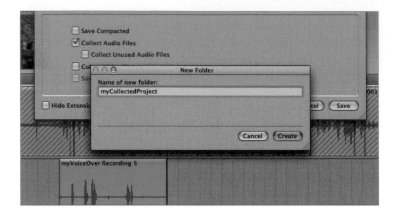

7   In the Save As dialog, click the Save button.

The Save As dialog is replaced by a progress bar showing Soundtrack Pro
collecting the project.

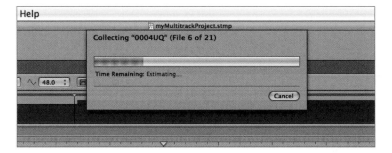

When the process is finished, you are left with a new project file, along
with a new Media folder that contains all of the audio files used in the
project. But that's not the best part—read on to the next step to find
out why.

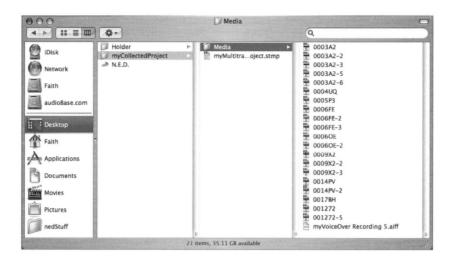

8   Click the File menu to open it and take a look at the options.

The Save command has turned into a Save (Collected) command. From now on, each time you save the project, all newly added audio files (including recordings) will be saved in your collected project folder.

Using Punch Recording

Before computer-based multitrack recording became commonplace, people recorded on analog tape. Lacking the incredible editing features we take for granted today, audio engineers of yore had to come up with some clever techniques for recording sound, and punch recording was one of them.

Punch recording occurs when you start recording as the project is playing. It gets its name from the old-school recording technique of starting playback on a tape-based editing system, and then literally punching (or pressing) the Record button to begin recording from a specific place in the song.

Even with today's powerful digital audio workstations, punch recording remains a valuable recording technique. Let's do some punch recording now, just to try the technique. You'll do so by recording over the last two "yeses" in your voiceover.

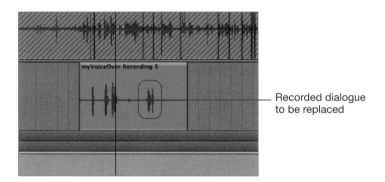

Recorded dialogue
to be replaced

1   Ensure that the myVoiceOver track is armed for recording.

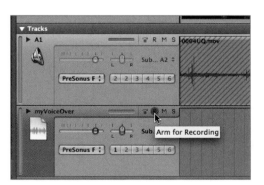

2   Use the Timecode HUD to move the playhead to 40 seconds into the audio clip.

3   Start playback.

4   As the playhead nears the final two "yeses," click the Record button and speak the words (this is called punching in).

5   Click the Record button to finish the punch recording (this is called punching out).

A newly recorded clip appears in the Timeline.

NOTE ▶ The newly recorded clip did not erase the audio that was there before. In fact, that audio is still under the new clip, so if you move or delete the new recording, the old recording is still there for you to work with.

6   Save your project.

Because you've already saved your work here as a collected project, the new recording is saved into the Media folder, along with the project's other audio files.

Lesson Review

1.   What is the Timecode HUD?

2.   Where is the Recording tab located?

3.   True or false: In Soundtrack Pro, you cannot record more than two channels of audio in the same clip.

4.   What level should you set as the peak for recording, and why?

5.   Why is it a good idea to collect a project after recording?

Answers

1.   The Timecode HUD is a floating window that lets you see and adjust the playhead's timecode position.

2.   The Recording tab is in Soundtrack Pro's right pane.

3.   False. Depending on your audio interface, you can record up to six channels of audio (5.1 surround sound) in a single clip.

4.   Set a peak recording level of –3 dB. This level maximizes your signal-to-noise ratio while still leaving a bit of headroom for unexpected loud parts of the recording.

5.   When you collect a project, all of the project's audio files are collected together and placed in a Media folder beside the new project file. All of the project's future recordings will also be collected in the new Media folder each time you save the project.

Keyboard Shortcuts

Command-T	Adds a track to a project
Shift-Command-T	Deletes a track from a project
Control-D	Shows or hides the right pane

5

Lesson Files   APTS-SoundtrackPro > Lesson 05 > 05 Begin.stmp

Time   This lesson takes approximately 30 minutes to complete.

Goals   Work with Soundtrack Pro's audio editing tools

Turn off snapping

Arrange clips in tracks

Nudge clips in the Timeline

Time stretch audio clips

Work with cycle regions

Adjust track and clip volume

Set and apply an ambient noise print

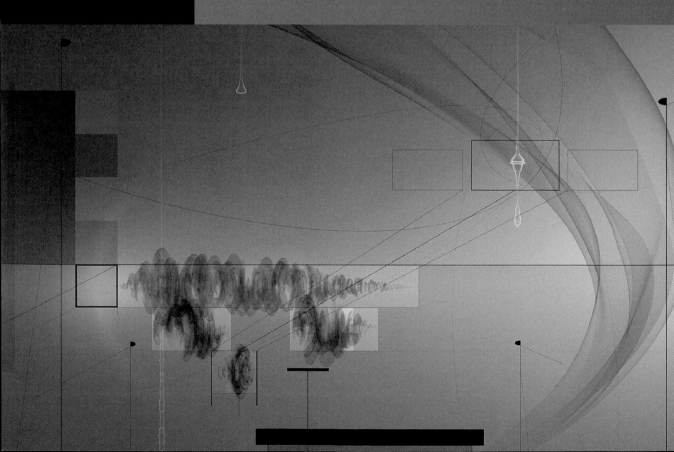

Old-School Dialogue Replacement

In the preceding lesson you made your first recording using Soundtrack Pro. Specifically, you used Soundtrack Pro's recording tools to record dialogue for a character in the **Blind Date** sequence. However, that procedure is far from finished. You still need to edit the waveform, cut off parts of the dialogue you don't need, and adjust the recording so your words match the movement of the onscreen actor's lips.

In this lesson you'll learn important audio editing techniques that will help you work with waveforms and clips to make the soundtracks in your mind a reality in Soundtrack Pro. Along the way, you'll learn the old-school method of dialogue replacement, which is a time-consuming process that involves deft skill with all of Soundtrack Pro's editing tools. However, it also provides great practice in using Soundtrack Pro's editing tools, so let's begin.

Using Soundtrack Pro's Editing Tools

In the upper-left corner of the Multitrack Editor is a toolbar that contains all of the tools you need to edit audio in Soundtrack Pro. Some of these tools, for example, the Selection (arrow) and Blade tools, will look familiar, because the same tools are used in Final Cut Pro. Others, such as the Timeslice and Lift tools, have specific functions that apply to Soundtrack Pro only. In either case, knowing the tools of your trade, and also how to use them, is an important part of becoming an efficient audio editor.

Using the Selection Tool

The Selection tool, also known as the arrow, is a multifaceted tool that does much more than just select clips. Indeed, you can also use it to move clips and edit the duration of clips by adjusting their left and right boundaries. The Selection tool is an important . . . er, arrow in your audio editing quiver, so let's notch the string and start shooting.

1   In Soundtrack Pro, open the project titled **05 Begin.stmp** or continue working on the Soundtrack Pro project you had open at the end of Lesson 4.

2   Click the Selection tool or press the A key on your keyboard, just like in Final Cut Pro.

3   In the myVoiceOver track, select the large **myVoiceOver** clip.

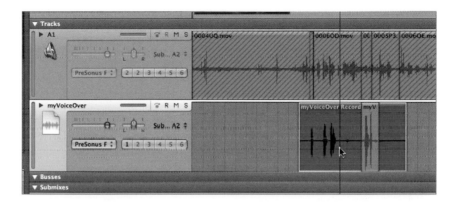

The clip turns dark green, indicating that it is selected. Notice that a portion of the selected clip extends beyond the smaller clip you punch recorded in the previous lesson. This is because the punch recording sits on top of the selected clip. At any point, you could select and move that smaller clip, and you would then be able to hear the audio in the clip underneath. This brings up an important point: *Soundtrack Pro always plays the audio in the clip on top (just as Final Cut Pro always plays the video clip on top), and mutes (does not play) the audio from the clip underneath.*

4   Position the pointer over the left edge of the clip.

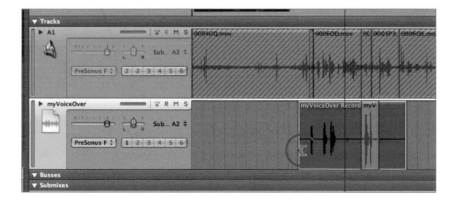

The arrow turns into a Clip Resize pointer.

5   With snapping turned off, drag toward the right to remove the "silence" at the beginning of the clip.

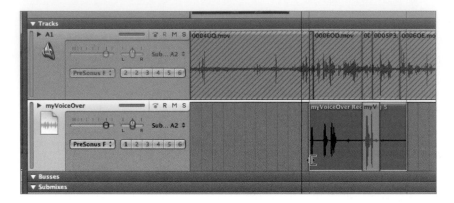

Of course, the section you've removed is not exactly silent; there is some ambient noise recorded by your microphone. However, the ambient noise in your dialogue does not match the ambient noise in the scene's original source audio, so as the audio engineer you have the responsibility to remove as much of the noise from your recording as possible so the recording fits snugly into the scene.

On this note, the edit you've just made is a bit loose. Let's use a trick to tighten it up a bit.

6   On your computer keyboard, press Option-Z (make sure the **myVoiceOver** clip is still selected before doing this).

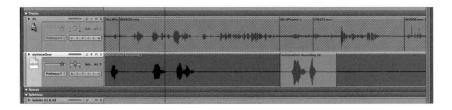

Soundtrack Pro automatically zooms so that the selected clip fills the Timeline. How cool is that? However, at this zoom level you can clearly see there is still a bit of the recording at the front of the clip that needs to be removed.

7   Drag the left edge of the clip until it stops at the beginning of the recorded vocal.

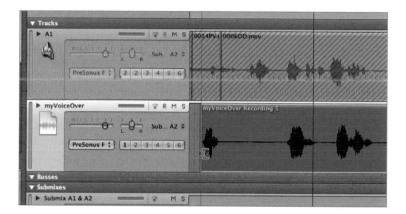

Using the Blade Tool

The Blade tool has one function only, but it's an important one—this tool is used to cut, or divide, clips in the Timeline.

1   Click the Blade tool (or press the B key on your keyboard, just like in Final Cut Pro).

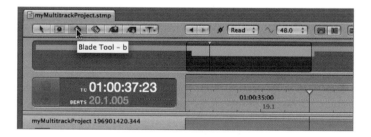

When you move the pointer back over the Timeline, it will now turn into a blade icon, indicating that the Blade tool is selected.

2   Click the selected clip directly behind the third set of "yes" recordings.

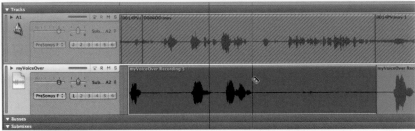

The clip is divided in two. You have just performed a split.

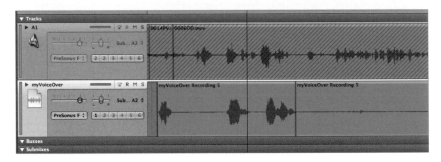

NOTE ▶ Soundtrack Pro also contains a Blade All tool that cuts across all clips in multiple tracks in the Timeline at once. The key command for this tool is BB (press the B key twice in quick succession).

Deleting Clips

In Soundtrack Pro you can delete clips by selecting them with the Selection tool and then pressing the Delete key on your keyboard, or you can use the following trick to delete clips with any tool you currently have selected.

1   With the Blade tool still selected, Control-click the clip to the right of the split you made in the steps above.

A shortcut menu appears.

2   From the shortcut menu, choose Delete.

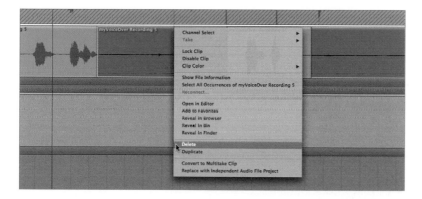

The selected clip is deleted.

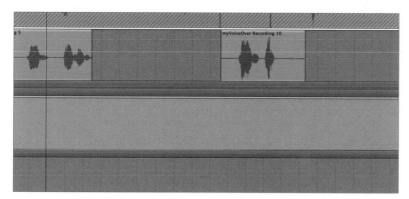

Using the Timeslice Tool

The Timeslice tool is a special selection tool that allows you to select portions of a clip, or even portions of multiple clips in the same track or on different tracks. This tool differs from the Selection tool in one important way: All selections made using the Timeslice tool are entirely time based. Unlike the normal Selection tool, which can select only entire clips at once, the Timeslice tool allows you to make exact edits to a small part of a clip without affecting the other parts of the selected clip.

1   Click the Timeslice tool (or press the W key on your keyboard).

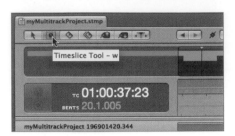

2   In the Timeline, drag a selection range over the "silence" between the first and second set of "yeses" in your recording.

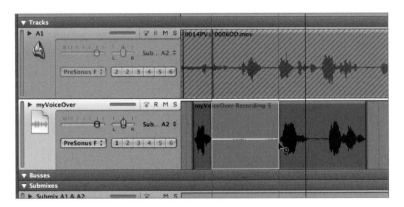

A portion of the clip is selected.

3   On your computer keyboard, press the Delete key.

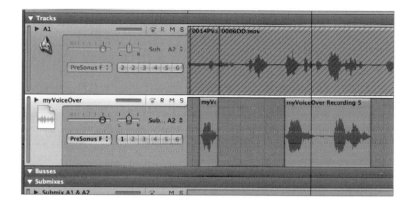

The selected portion of the clip is deleted.

Editing Tools Exercise

The Selection, Blade, and Timeslice tools are important tools, so take a moment to exercise your editing skills by trimming the rest of your recording to remove any excess noise.

Use the editing techniques demonstrated in this section to edit your recording so the clips in the myVoiceOver track look similar to the following figure.

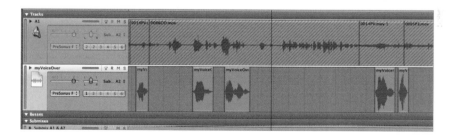

Arranging Clips

In the previous section you used Soundtrack Pro's editing tools to cut out portions of your recording that are not needed for your voiceover. However, unless you were spot on in your vocal recording, your words probably don't match up exactly with the movement of the onscreen actor's lips. In this section, you'll explore techniques for moving clips in one track, and also across multiple tracks, to create a more precise arrangement.

Snapping Mode

In the following steps, you will make very fine adjustments to the position of clips in your Timeline. However, by default Soundtrack Pro has snapping enabled. Snapping is a great feature if you are aligning musical loops to create a song, or adjusting clips to marker positions as you spot sounds to your score, but when it comes time to make fine adjustments to clip positions in your project, snapping is not a helpful feature. You'll learn a lot more about snapping later in this book, but for now, make sure that snapping is turned off.

> **NOTE** ▶ To temporarily toggle snapping, press the Command key as you move clips. If snapping is turned on, it will temporarily turn off while the Command key is pressed. If snapping is off, it will turn on while the Command key is pressed.

1   Move any clip left or right in the Timeline.

Notice that the clip snaps from grid point to grid point.

2   Press Command-Z to undo the move.

3   Choose View > Snap (N) and make sure the snapping mode is off.

If there's a checkmark to the left of the word *Snap*, then snapping mode is on. No checkmark means snapping is turned off, and that's a good thing for the steps that follow.

4   Move a clip in the Timeline.

Notice that the clip now moves smoothly between grid points.

5   Press Command-Z to undo the move.

Moving Clips in a Single Track

These days, audio editing is as much a visual process as it is an auditory one, and that's great if, like most video editors, you are a visual person. For example, if you look closely at the waveforms in your tracks, you can clearly see the blocks of sound that make up the spoken words in this soundtrack. If you look carefully at the waveforms, you will see that your recorded "yeses" look strikingly similar to the onscreen actor's recorded "yeses." In fact, the similarities are so apparent you can often achieve great lip sync by simply lining up your newly recorded waveforms with the old waveforms from the source audio file.

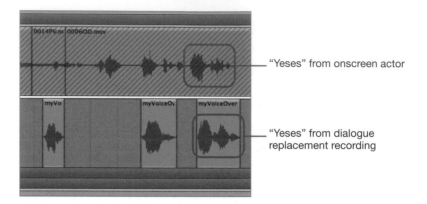

"Yeses" from onscreen actor

"Yeses" from dialogue replacement recording

With this in mind, it's a fairly simple process to lock the lip sync in your dialogue replacement recording. Let's move the newly recorded clips to line them up with the source recording.

> **NOTE** ▶ No two recordings are ever exactly the same, so your recording is going to look a bit different from the recording in the figures that follow. Keep that in mind as you read through the following steps.

1   Look at the waveforms in your Timeline and determine which clips need to be moved to align the dialogue recordings.

2   Click the Selection Tool button (or press A on your keyboard).

3   Click a clip to select it.

4   Drag the clip left or right until its left edge begins at the same point as the beginning of the waveform it will eventually replace.

Alignment guides

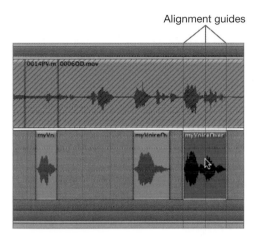

As you drag, notice that three alignment guides appear, one on the left edge of the clip, one on the right edge, and one directly aligned with the point on the clip you clicked when you initiated the drag process. Pay particular attention to the left alignment guide and make sure the left edge of your dialogue recording matches the left edge of the waveform representing the onscreen actor's words.

5   Click the Timeline just before the edit you've made to reposition the playhead.

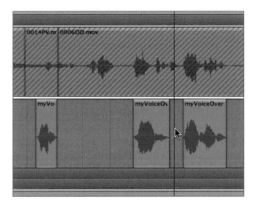

6   Press the spacebar to play the project and listen to the edit.

Do your words match up?

7   Press the spacebar again to stop playback.

8   Repeat steps 3 through 7 to adjust the position of the other dialogue clips in your recording. Don't worry about positioning them perfectly at this point; we'll nudge the clips into place in the next exercise.

Nudging Clips Frame by Frame

Ensuring that your recorded dialogue is in sync with the lip movement of the onscreen actor is an important part of dialogue replacement, and sometimes even the smallest adjustments to clip position can make all the difference in the world to your project. In these situations, nudging clips frame by frame is a perfect way to align the spoken words with the sound from your characters.

1   Choose a dialogue clip that is marginally out of sync with the onscreen actor's lip movement. (If your dialogue recording is perfectly in sync, just select any clip for the following steps. You can nudge it back after you learn the technique.)

2   Do one of the following:

▶   To nudge the clip left one video frame, press Command–Option–Left Arrow.

▶   To nudge the clip right one video frame, press Command–Option–Right Arrow.

Adjusting Clip Duration

Let's be realistic: chances are that some of your recorded words last either a bit longer or shorter than the words being spoken by the onscreen actor, so the durations of your recorded words don't exactly match the duration of the words in the source file. The next figure demonstrates a good example of this. Notice how the recorded dialogue waveform and onscreen actor's word start at the same point in time, yet the recorded dialogue clip is longer than the waveform in the source audio file.

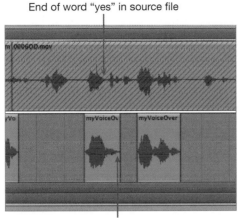

End of word "yes" in source file

End of word "yes" in dialogue recording

Happily, Soundtrack Pro contains great time-stretching features you can use to fix little issues like this. Time stretching is the process of adjusting the duration of an audio clip without affecting the clip's pitch. In other words, you can use Soundtrack Pro to seamlessly adjust the duration of a clip, without affecting the way the clip sounds. (Note that very extreme stretching will distort sound.) The steps below show you how.

1   If the lower pane is not visible, click the Lower Pane button in the upper-right corner of the Toolbar.

2   In the Timeline, select a clip with a duration that needs adjusting.

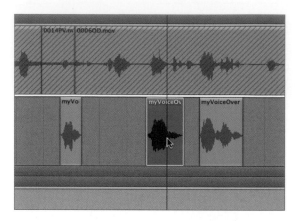

3   In the lower pane, click the File Editor tab.

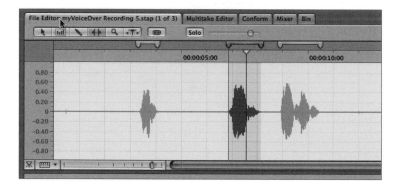

Does this pane look familiar? It should, because this is essentially a version of the File Editor that you've seen and used in previous lessons, except it exists right here in the lower pane of Soundtrack Pro's workspace. You can do all of the same edits in the File Editor tab as you can in the File Editor itself, without the need to launch a separate project in your workspace. How handy is that?

4 From the File Editor tab's toolbar, select the Audio Stretching tool ('I').

5 With the Audio Stretching tool, drag a selection range over the audio you want to stretch.

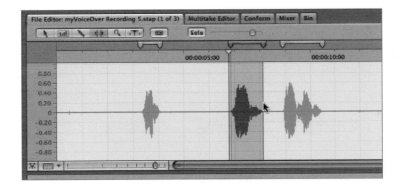

A selection range appears, with purple lines on its left and right edges.

6 Position the Audio Stretching tool over the purple line on the right edge of the selected audio.

Stretch pointer

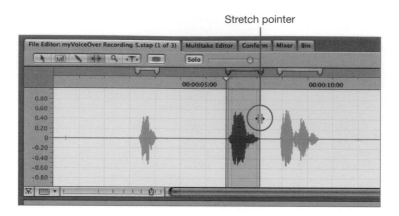

The arrow turns into the Stretch pointer.

7   Drag left or right (depending on whether you are shortening or lengthening the duration) to resize the selected portion of the audio file.

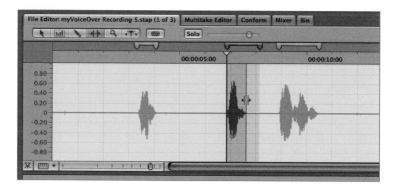

The selected area of the audio file is stretched. Back in the Timeline, you can clearly see the results of your edit and judge if your edit is correct.

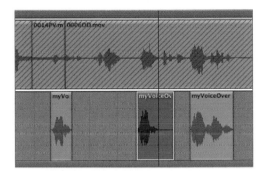

8 In the left pane, click the Actions tab.

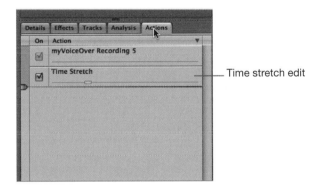

— Time stretch edit

Notice that your time stretch edit is added to the Actions list. You can easily undo this edit at any time, by just toggling it off, or even deleting it from the Actions list.

Admittedly, this edit could take a few tries, as there are no precise markers in the File Editor tab to show you exactly where the audio should be stretched to. But that's fine, because good audio editing always takes time and refinement.

9 Play your project and listen to the edit you've made.

10 If necessary, repeat steps 5 through 7 above until the clip is exactly the correct duration.

11 If there are other clips in your project that need to be time stretched, select them and repeat steps 5 through 7 until they are all perfectly aligned with the original source audio.

Truncating Overlapping Clips

At the moment, there are two versions of every "yes" playing when you audition the project: one from your dialogue recording, and one from the onscreen actor. That's too many "yeses," so let's get rid of the original "yeses" using Soundtrack Pro's truncate mode.

But first, let's do a little bit of cleanup. When you stretched your audio clips in the previous exercise, you probably created some "dead audio" space at the end of your tightly edited clips. For example, the clip in the figure below has had silence added to its end. We don't need this silence, so let's remove it before truncating the original audio.

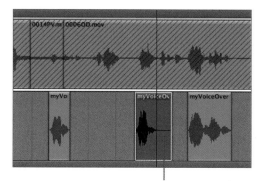

Silence added to end of clip from time stretching

1 Click the Selection Tool button (A).

2   Adjust the right edge of any clip that needs the silence removed (for more information about working with clips, see the section above titled "Using the Selection Tool").

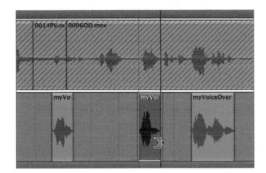

3   Using the Selection tool, drag across all of the clips in your dialogue recording track to select them.

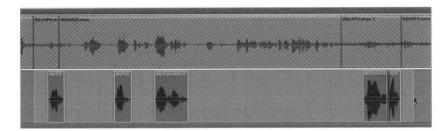

4   At the top of the Timeline, click the Truncate button.

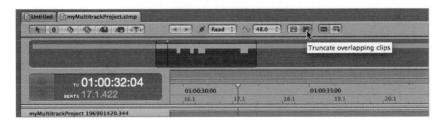

You are about to edit the audio in your source track, but that track is currently locked. Let's unlock it now so you can make your next edit.

5   Control-click the header of track A1, and choose Unlock Selected Track from the shortcut menu.

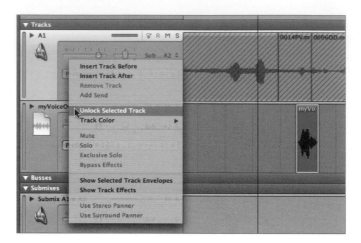

The diagonal lines across track A1 are removed, indicating the track is no longer locked and may now be edited. OK, the next shot is for all the marbles, so pay attention and proceed carefully.

6   Press and hold down the Shift key, and then drag the selected clips from your dialogue recording track up to track A1.

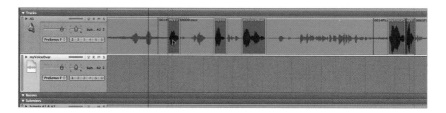

Holding down the Shift key as you move clips between tracks forces Soundtrack Pro to move the clips linearly, in one direction only. In other words, you have just moved the clips up vertically, without fear that you might lose sync by accidentally moving the clips horizontally as well. This in turn ensures that all of your careful edits will remain in exactly the same time position in your project.

7   Hold down the Shift key and move the selected clips back down to the dialogue recording track.

Presto! Where once there was audio, there are now empty spaces containing no sound. And that's just great, because it means all of those extraneous "yeses" from the onscreen actor have now been removed.

8   Play the project and listen to the edits you've made.

We're getting close to a good dialogue replacement, but admittedly there are a few issues that still need to be addressed. For example, the sound of the background noise from the scene is absent from the new dialogue recordings. Additionally, the volume of your recorded dialogue probably does not mix well with the volume of the original recording. Let's move on to the next section to make these small adjustments.

Mixing the Recording into the Scene

The dialogue clips you've recorded need to be adjusted so they fit into the mix. Right now they are probably a bit too loud, so let's examine a few techniques for working with volume in Soundtrack Pro.

Creating a Cycle Region

When trying to match the volume between two tracks, it often helps to create a *cycle region* so that you can hear the audio play repeatedly while you make your volume adjustment. It's a simple trick, and it allows your ears to become accustomed to the sound.

1   In the Time ruler at the top of the Timeline, drag from left to right to create a cycle region around the area of the Timeline that contains the first three "yeses."

Click here   Drag to here

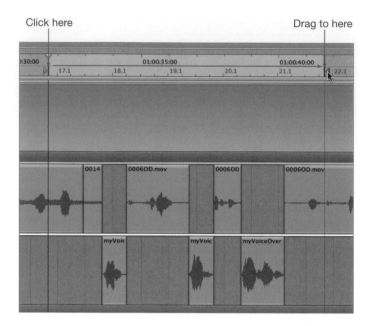

Soundtrack Pro sets In and Out points in the Timeline. This isn't rocket science, so don't worry about creating a cycle of an exact length. As long as the In and Out points encompass the first three "yeses" as shown in the figure above, you're golden.

2   In the transport controls at the bottom of Soundtrack Pro's workspace, click the Cycle button (or press the C key on your keyboard).

3   Press the spacebar to play your project.

As the project plays, notice it automatically loops from the Out point back to the In point. Your project is cycling!

4 Press the spacebar to stop playback.

Adjusting Track Volume

The volume of your recorded dialogue needs to be adjusted so that it fits with the volume of the clips around it. This is the point where you really must put on your audio engineer's hat and depend on your ears more than your eyes. Listen carefully as you work through the steps below.

1 Press the spacebar to start the playback of your cycle.

2 As the cycle plays, adjust the volume slider on the track header.

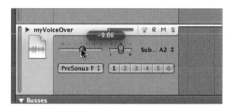

Moving the slider left decreases the volume, while moving the slider right increases the volume.

3 When you have set the volume so that the recorded dialogue blends evenly with the source audio, press the spacebar to stop playback.

Using Actions to Adjust Clip Volume

While the track volume slider will typically be the first place you stop to adjust the volume of a clip, you can also adjust volume using actions. This is particularly important to keep in mind in situations where you need to apply a volume adjustment *before* an action is applied, because any changes made using the track volume slider occur *after* the actions are applied to the clip(s) in question.

Both techniques are important to know, so let's undo the volume adjustment from the last step and check out an alternative technique for applying volume (amplitude) changes to a clip.

1 Hover the pointer over the voiceover track's volume slider.

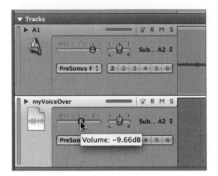

A tooltip appears and displays the slider's setting. Pay attention to this number, because you'll need it a few steps from now. Let's return the volume slider to its factory default setting of 0 dB. You could do this by just dragging the slider as outlined in the steps above, but there's a better way, so keep reading.

2 Double-click anywhere on the volume slider.

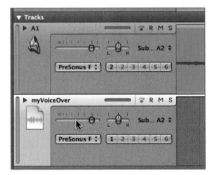

The slider jumps to its default setting of 0 dB. Remember this trick, because double-clicking any slider or control in Soundtrack Pro returns that slider or control to its default position.

3   In the Timeline, select the first ADR or VoiceOver clip.

The File Editor tab is still open in the lower pane, so the audio file appears there; the region representing the clip is selected. However, the volume change we applied to the track affects every clip in the track, and several clips are part of this one audio file. Consequently, you need to apply the volume change to the *entire file* to ensure that each clip's volume is properly adjusted.

4   Click anywhere on the File Editor tab to make sure it is in focus.

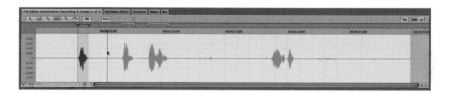

5   Press Command-A to select the *entire* audio file.

6   Choose Process > Adjust Amplitude.

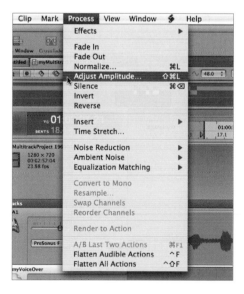

The Adjust Amplitude dialog appears. You can use this function to adjust the volume of the audio file, through actions.

7   In the number field on the right of the Adjust Amplitude dialog, enter the value that was set on the volume slider from step 1, and click OK.

NOTE ▸ If you attenuated, or lowered, the volume of your track, make sure you put a minus (–) in front of the input volume so Soundtrack Pro knows to decrease the volume. Positive values will increase the volume.

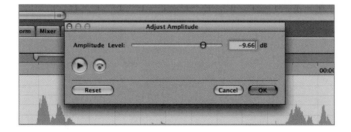

Soundtrack Pro adjusts the volume of the entire audio file, which includes all Timeline clips that are part of the audio file. To prove this, follow the next step.

8   In the Timeline, select any of the first three audio clips in the voiceover track.

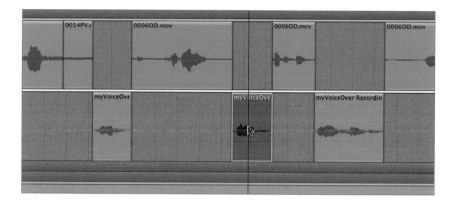

9 Click the Actions tab in the left pane.

Notice that the Adjust Amplitude action has been applied to the clip. Furthermore, the "bar" representing the part of the clip to which the action has been applied covers the entire clip, and not just a certain section. Consequently, you can tell the action has been applied to the entire clip!

10 Press the spacebar to play the cycle region you defined a couple of sections ago.

As you can hear, the volume has been adjusted, using actions.

NOTE ▶ You can change the volume assigned to this action by double-clicking the Adjust Amplitude action in the Actions list and changing the volume assigned to the action.

Working with Ambient Noise

With the volume adjusted, you can now clearly hear how your dialogue clips lack the ambient noise of the source audio stream. Indeed, the change in ambient noise between your recordings and the source audio is abrupt and noticeable. For example, the first recorded "yes" comes in just as a motorcycle passes by, offscreen. The roar of the motorcycle can be heard, but it stops instantly when the recorded "yes" occurs.

In the real world, this would happen only if the motorcycle hit a wall, but then we'd also have the sound of a large crash to accompany the abruptly ending sound. This does not occur in our scene, and consequently the sound is not natural. That's a bit of a problem, so let's use a handy Soundtrack Pro process to quickly fix this issue.

The sound of the motorcycle in this clip ends abruptly.

1 In track A1, select the clip containing the sound of the motorcycle.

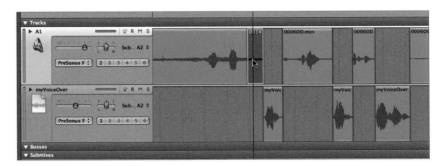

2   Choose Process > Ambient Noise > Set Ambient Noise Print (Control-Command-Y).

Soundtrack Pro uses the sound in the clip as the basis for an *ambient noise print*.

NOTE ▸ You can also select just a portion of a file for an ambient noise print by opening the file in the lower pane's File Editor tab and selecting whichever portion you want to use for the ambient noise print. This helps in situations where a clip contains, for example, both ambient noise you want to use, and sounds such as dialogue, which you don't.

3 In the voiceover track, select the first "yes" clip.

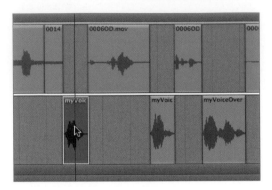

4 Choose Process > Ambient Noise > Add Ambient Noise (Command-Y).

The ambient noise lifted from the first clip is applied to the second clip, and the transition into the recorded dialogue clip is now seamless, with no abrupt end to the sound of the motorcycle passing by the scene.

5   Ensure that the Actions tab is displayed in the left pane.

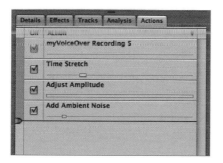

Notice that Add Ambient Noise is added to the clip as an action. If you need to remove or modify this noise print later on, well, you know the methods by now. . .

TIP The Process > Ambient Noise menu contains a command called Replace With Ambient Noise. Choosing this option directly replaces the selected clip (or portion of a clip) with whatever sound is contained in the ambient noise print. This can come in handy, for example, if you have a scene with several expletives you need to bleep out. Just import a "bleep" sound somewhere in your project, set it as the noise print, and then select and replace all the words you need to bleep out, with the ambient noise print.

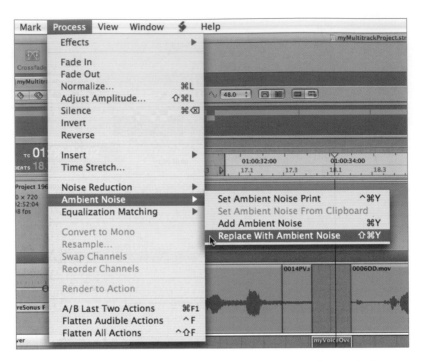

Use the Replace With Ambient Noise command to bleep expletives and other unwanted words out of questionable scenes.

Lesson Review

1. What are the key commands for the Selection (arrow) and Blade tools, respectively?

2. True or false: The Timeslice tool can be used to select portions of clips, whereas the Selection tool can select only entire clips.

3. How do you time stretch an audio clip?

4. How do you create a cycle region?

5. What is an ambient noise print?

Answers

1. A for the Selection tool, and B for the Blade tool.

2. True.

3. Select the clip to open it in the File Editor, then use the Audio Stretching tool to select a portion (or all) of the clip. Finally, use the Stretch pointer to drag the edges of the selected clip to the correct duration.

4. Drag horizontally in the Time ruler at the top of the Timeline to create In and Out points defining the cycle region, then click the Cycle button (C) in the transport controls to activate the cycle region.

5. An ambient noise print is a section of audio you define and set by choosing Process > Ambient Noise > Set Ambient Noise Print. Once the ambient noise print is set, you can apply it to any clip in your project, and Soundtrack Pro will mix the ambient noise print with the sounds already contained in the selected clip.

6

New-School Dialogue Replacement

Dialogue replacement is a key feature of Soundtrack Pro, and the latest version of the software makes it easier than ever to sync studio-recorded dialogue with field-recorded video. In the previous two lessons, you got a taste for the "old school" method of dialogue replacement, which involves a lot of cutting, shifting, nudging, time stretching, and other techniques. In the olden days (which is the present time for most audio editing DAWs), dialogue replacement was a time-consuming process that involved attention to detail and much patience.

But with Soundtrack Pro you are part of the new school when it comes to dialogue replacement. The previous two lessons were a good exercise in how things used to be done, and you gained solid experience using Soundtrack Pro's audio editing tools to record, trim, arrange, and otherwise edit clips in the Timeline. But now you're about to experience something special: Soundtrack Pro's Multitake Editor.

The Multitake Editor allows you to record several takes into one clip in the Timeline. You'll also be able to mix parts of each take to create a final composite clip that will fool the eyes and ears of all but the most discerning of video viewers.

About Cycle Recording

Cycle recording—that is, recording multiple takes of a cycle region—is an old-school technique that almost every DAW can do. You simply create a cycle region (as you did in Lesson 5) and then start recording. As the cycle loops from its end to the beginning, the DAW creates a new recording for each pass through the cycle. In most other DAWs, each new "take" is added to the timeline on its own individual track, which means at the end of a long cycle recording session, you end up with several tracks, sometimes even dozens of tracks, littering your timeline. Soundtrack Pro avoids this timeline congestion by placing all the takes inside a single clip.

Setting Up for Cycle Recording

Before you can do any cycle recording, you need to have an empty track ready to record to.

1 In the Lesson 06 folder, open the file titled **06 Begin.stmp**, or continue working on your project from the previous lesson.

2 On the myVoiceOver track, click the Mute (M) button.

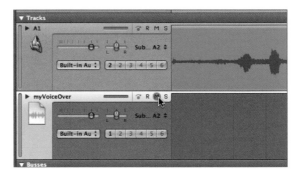

The track is grayed out and will no longer play. This allows you to concentrate fully on the recordings you are about to make, without getting confused by your previous recording. However, you still need a track to record to.

3 Control-click in the track header for the myVoiceOver track, and choose Insert Track Before in the shortcut menu that appears.

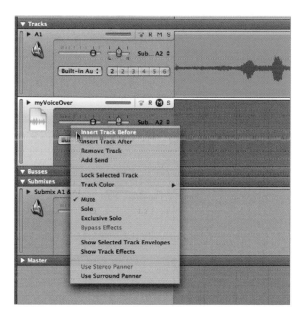

Soundtrack Pro creates a new track above the myVoiceOver track.

4   Name the new track *Multitake*.

Now you're ready to record. In the next section you'll create your first cycle recording.

Cycle Recording

The process of cycle recording is a simple one. Soundtrack Pro takes care of all the heavy lifting, leaving you to focus on getting the best possible signal into Soundtrack Pro.

For the following exercise, record three or four different passes, or takes, of the voiceover "yeses."

1   If you continue working on your project from Lesson 5, make sure you have a cycle region covering the first three "yeses" in the sequence.

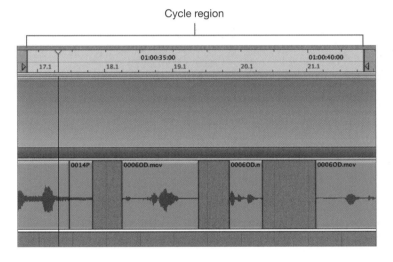

The exact duration of the cycle region is immaterial, as long as it encompasses the first three "yeses" in the project. In fact, you should already have defined a cycle region in the Timeline from the last lesson, so you can probably skip this step. If you need more information on creating a cycle region, please see the section in Lesson 5 titled "Creating a Cycle Region."

2   On the Multitake track, click the Arm for Recording button.

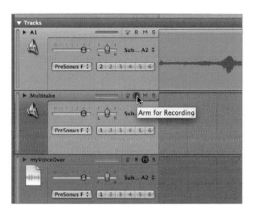

With the track armed for recording, you need to ensure that it is properly configured. For example, by default the track is set to record a stereo signal, but your microphone is probably a mono signal source, so you will need to change that.

3   Click the right pane's Recording tab and make sure the Multitake track is properly set up for recording. For more details, see Lesson 4, "Recording in Soundtrack Pro."

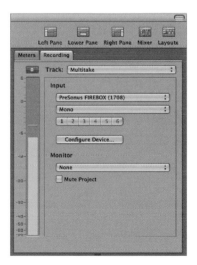

You're now ready to cycle record.

4 Turn off your monitor speakers and put on your headphones. You don't want any signal feeding back into your microphone, so be careful.

5 On Soundtrack Pro's transport controls, click the Record button (or press the R key).

Soundtrack Pro begins recording. Watch the video in the left pane's Video tab, and record your voiceover "yeses." Let Soundtrack Pro do at least three or four passes to ensure you have a good number of alternative takes to work with.

6 When you've finished recording three or four takes, press the spacebar to stop recording.

A new clip appears in the Multitake track.

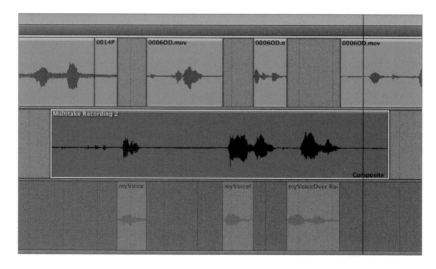

Even more important, the Multitake Editor tab jumps into focus in the lower pane. A close look at the Multitake Editor shows that all of your takes—the passes recorded in cycle recording mode—are represented by individual tracks in the clip.

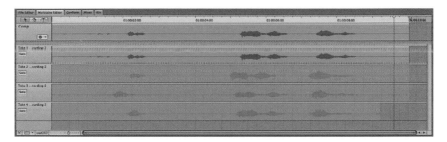

MORE INFO ▶ A multitake clip is sort of like a nested sequence in Final Cut Pro. The clip in the Timeline is like the nested clip, while the Multitake Editor is like stepping into the nest, where you can see all of the stacked tracks that make up the nested clip. Like all other nested sequences, the edits and modifications performed inside the nest are reflected in the parent clip in the Timeline.

The Multitake Editor

The Multitake Editor is designed to make it easy for you to juggle multiple voiceover recordings. Using the Multitake Editor, you can mix the good parts of each take and omit the bad parts. In fact, the Multitake Editor is like a small multitrack editor built into a single audio clip. You can slip portions of audio back and forth to improve the lip sync, and even crossfade between different takes to make smooth transitions that will fool all but the most discerning ears (and probably some of those, too). In the end, you are left with a "comp," a composite take that you can use and edit in the Timeline like any other clip in your project.

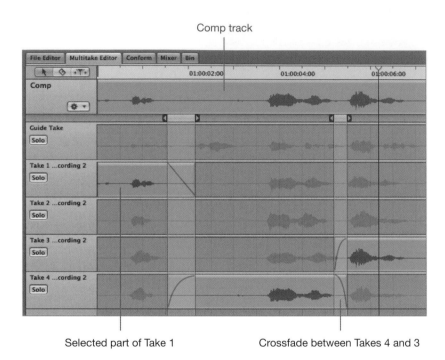

Selected part of Take 1   Crossfade between Takes 4 and 3

Adding a Prerecorded Take

In the following steps, you will add a *guide track* to the Multitake Editor. A guide track is an audio file containing the audio from the original source. With a guide track in place, you can use the shape of the waveforms from the original audio to more accurately position your newly recorded voiceover.

NOTE ▸ Alternatively, you can use the steps below to add takes that were recorded in a different studio to compile a multitake clip.

1 In the Lesson 6 folder, go to **guideTake.aif**.

2 Drag the **guideTake.aif** file to anywhere on the Multitake Editor tab.

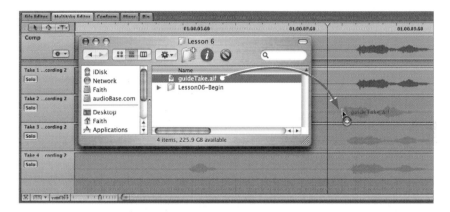

A new take is added to the bottom of the Multitake Editor.

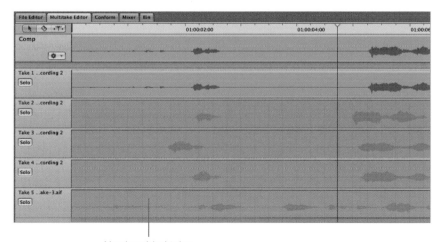

Newly added take

NOTE ▶ You can also add a take by choosing Add Take from the pop-up menu in the Comp track header. From the same pop-up menu you can also remove takes you don't need.

Naming Takes

If you've got a lot of takes in the Multitake Editor, you may want to name them so you can keep them straight. Here's how you do it.

1 In the header of the newly added take track, click the name.

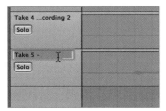

A text field appears.

2 Type *Guide Take* and press Return.

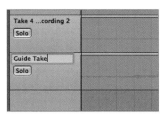

The take is renamed.

Reordering Takes

The Guide Take track is currently at the bottom of the Multitake Editor. However, we want to use it as a guide to help us position the words in our voiceover, so let's move it to the top of the Multitake Editor.

1 Drag the header of the Guide Take track until it's above the other takes in the Multitake Editor.

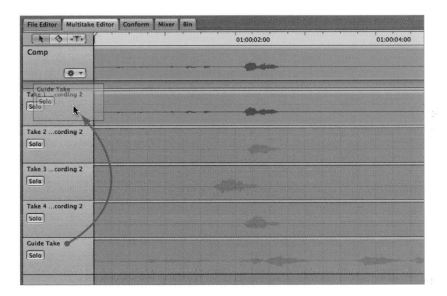

The take is moved to the top of the Multitake Editor.

Auditioning Takes

The active take, or the one that is playing, always appears in a brighter green, while the muted takes have a much more muted color to them, indicating they will not be heard. By default, the first take in the Multitake Editor is the one that plays, but you can choose to play any take by simply clicking it. For now, you need to select the Guide Take track to ensure that it is the one you hear.

1   In the Multitake Editor, click anywhere on the Guide Take track.

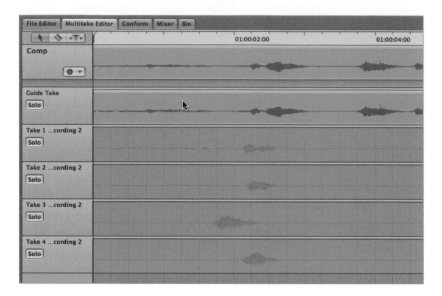

The Guide Take is selected and the other takes become muted.

2   Press the spacebar to play the cycle region.

You can now hear the Guide Take playing. However, you can also probably hear that the Guide Take is out of sync with the project audio. For example, notice where the female character says "I'm Carolyn" in each of the two tracks. Move these two areas so they are in sync. Do so by sight first, and then refine the edit using your ears (remember, you learned how to move and nudge clips in the last lesson, but more on that in a moment).

"I'm Carolyn" from project

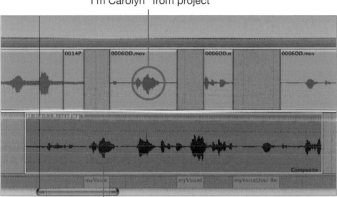

"I'm Carolyn" from Guide Take

3   Use the editing tricks you picked up in Lesson 5, including selecting, moving, and nudging, to perfectly align the "I'm Carolyn" words from the two tracks.

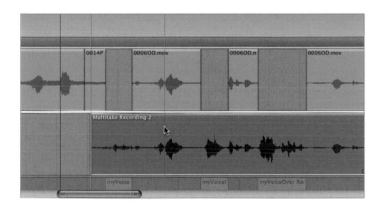

When the words are aligned, you will hear some interesting sounds as the words from the two tracks "phase" each other. This always occurs when two identical waveforms are *nearly* aligned, so that's a good sign! Don't worry about this phasing sound for now, because you will be removing the Guide Take in a few minutes, leaving nothing but your perfectly aligned takes.

Slipping Takes

Currently, the Guide Take is out of sync with your recorded takes. For example, the first "yes" is close to the beginning of the Guide Take, but your recorded takes probably start a little bit later.

First "yes" in Guide Take

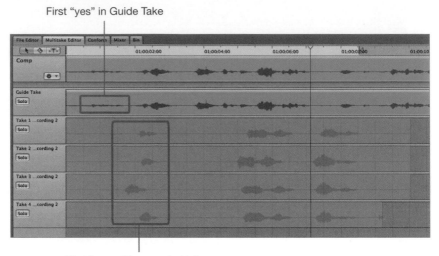

First "yeses" in recorded takes

To move the recorded takes into closer sync, you need to "slip" them along the Multitake Editor Timeline. In video editor's jargon, a slip edit occurs when you shift the position of your media left or right inside a clip, without changing the In or Out points of the clip itself in relation to the Timeline. In other words, the clip stays in its same time position in the Timeline, and no transitions or adjacent clips are affected, but the media inside the clip change position. To do a slip edit, follow these steps.

1   Command-Option-click the take track under the Guide Take (Take 1).

2   Continue pressing Option-Command and drag the take track left or right until the first "yes" waveform in Take 1 roughly aligns with the "yes" waveform in the Guide Take track.

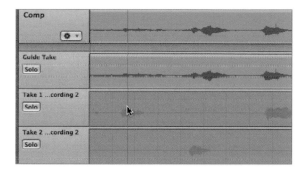

Don't worry about being exact; just try to get the edit close. You'll refine the edit for a closer lip sync as you work through the rest of this lesson.

3   Repeat steps 1 and 2 to slip the other takes into rough alignment with the Guide Take.

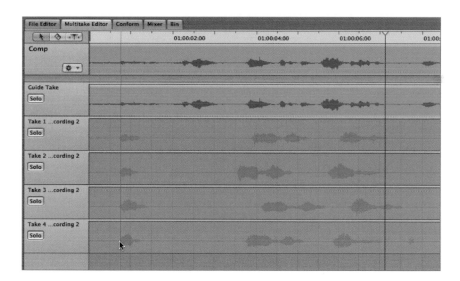

Creating a Composite Take

The main advantage of the Multitake Editor is that it allows you to assemble a composite, or master, take from regions of the other takes in the Multitake Editor. The Comp track is the one at the top of the editor, and it always displays the waveform of the sound that will play in the final project. To create a composite take, you split, slip, and select portions of the other takes as described in the steps below.

Splitting Takes

The process of splitting takes divides the takes in the Multitake Editor into discrete regions you can select to make the final composite. To split a take, you use the Multitake Editor's Blade tool.

1   In the Multitake Editor, select the Blade tool (B).

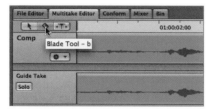

2   With the Blade tool, click after the first "yes" in the Guide Take track.

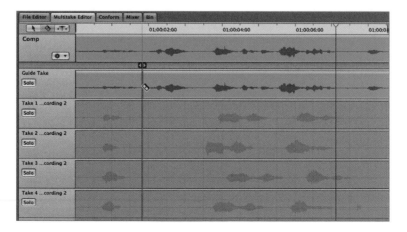

A transition point is created, and each take track, including the Guide Take track, is split into two regions. In essence, the Blade tool here acts like the Razor Blade All tool in Final Cut Pro, cutting a vertical line through all the takes in the Multitake Editor.

3   Using the Blade tool, click before the third "yes" in the Guide Take track.

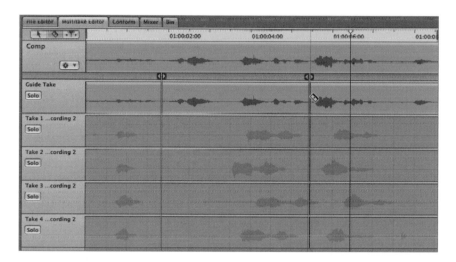

Each track is split into three regions.

4   In the Multitake Editor, click the Selection Tool button (A).

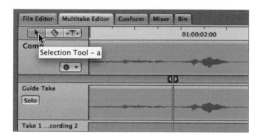

5   Slip the "yeses" region of each take track until all the "yeses" are roughly in line with the "yeses" in the Guide Take track (for more information, see the section above titled "Slipping Takes").

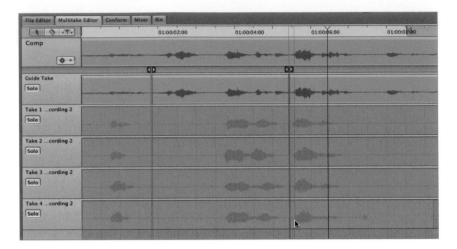

At this point, you can visually see that the "yeses" from your recorded takes are more or less in line with the "yeses" from the Guide Take. You'll probably need to refine these edits further in a moment, but for the time being, you can move on to the next exercise.

Selecting Takes

Now that you've split the takes into regions and slipped the recorded take tracks so they are more or less aligned with the Guide Take track, you need to select which part of each take will be used in the final composite.

1   Press the spacebar to play the cycle region.

The cycle region begins playing. Pay close attention to the next step, because it is a bit complex.

2   As the cycle plays, click the different regions of each take, listen closely, and watch the Video tab to see which takes sound the best and are in closest sync with the lip movements of the onscreen actor.

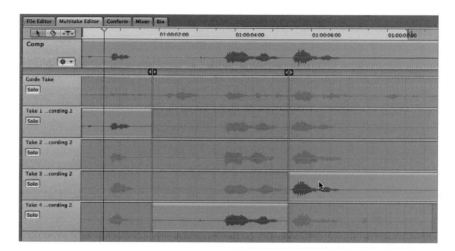

As you click different regions of the takes, each one in turn becomes the "active" take and the Comp track at the top of the Multitake Editor updates to display the waveform of the selected regions. The Multitake Editor makes it extremely easy to juggle multiple takes so that you get the best possible voiceover every time.

3   If necessary, slip the selected regions to move them closer into lip sync with the onscreen actor (for more information, see the section above titled "Slipping Takes").

Using Transitions

By now, you're probably convinced that the Multitake Editor makes dialogue replacement an easy process—much easier than the old-school method detailed in Lesson 5. But just when you thought things were good, they get even better! The Multitake Editor also includes a feature you can use to create fades between different takes. Let's check it out now.

Adding Transitions

A transition is a smooth fade between two pieces of media. As a video editor, you use transitions constantly to fade from black to your video, or from one clip to the next in a sequence. Audio transitions work much the same way, except you fade between two separate bits of sound. If you are performing tight edits to a multitake voiceover track, transitions can make the difference between sketchy dialogue replacement and smooth dialogue replacement that sounds as if it had been recorded while the scene was shot. Here's how it works.

1   At the top of the first transition point, where you split the take with the Blade tool, drag the arrow handles left and right to spread them apart.

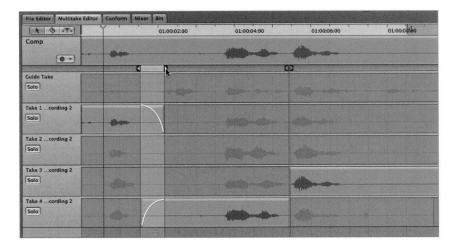

This creates a crossfade. Notice the fade lines that show you how the end of the first region will fade into the beginning of the second region. You'll learn about these fades in the next section. But your next step is to make a transition for the second split.

2   At the top of the second transition point, drag the arrow handles left and right to spread them apart.

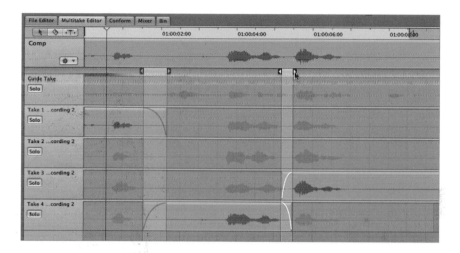

Working with Fades

A noted above, a transition is a smooth fade between two separate pieces of media. You can see the fades graphically displayed in the transitions you added above. Soundtrack Pro comes with several types of fades you can use. Let's explore these fade types now.

1   Double-click directly under the fade line in the first crossfade.

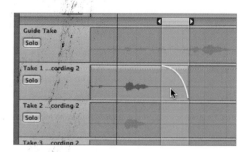

The Fade Selector appears. Down the left edge of the Fade Selector are four types of fades.

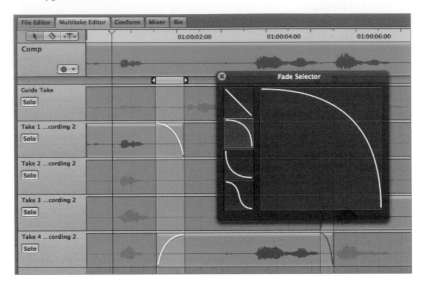

2   Select the type of fade that you require (for more information about fade types, see Lesson 7).

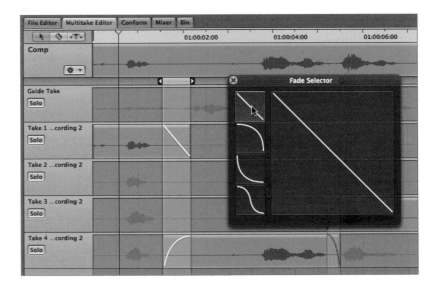

3   In the upper-left corner of the Fade Selector, click the close button.

The Fade Selector closes.

4   Repeat steps 1 through 3 to adjust the remaining fades in the Multitake Editor.

NOTE ▸ You can change the length of your fades at any time by positioning the pointer over the fade's left or right edge, and dragging.

Lesson Review

1.   How do you create a cycle recording?

2.   What does cycle recording do?

3.   What is the function of the Multitake Editor?

4.   In the Multitake Editor, what is a transition?

5.   True or false: You cannot change the default fade in the Multitake Editor's transitions.

Answers

1.   Set up a cycle region, record-enable a track, and click the Record button.

2.   Each time the cycle loops from the Out point back to the In point, Soundtrack Pro records a new take into the clip. These takes are visible in the Multitake Editor.

3.   The Multitake Editor lets you mix and match parts of different takes to ensure that you create the best possible composite take.

4.   A transition is a smooth fade from one take to the next.

5.   False: You can select among four types of fades for Multitake Editor transitions.

7

Lesson Files APTS-SoundtrackPro > Lesson 07 > 07 Begin.fcp

Media Lesson 7 > Media > SI HAND PROPPING CUB-a.mov

Lesson 7 > Media > 16R P51 two fly bys

Time This lesson takes approximately 30 minutes to complete.

Goals Use various techniques for spotting sound effects to the Timeline

Explore the Bin and the Browser

Use the Multipoint Video HUD

Create a three-point edit

Explore fade-ins and fade-outs

Use volume envelopes to create a custom fade

Lesson 7
Spotting Sound Effects

In previous chapters we've spent a lot of time discussing dialogue in Soundtrack Pro, and that's important stuff, because dialogue is the main source of auditory information in any video production. Consequently, viewers spend more time focusing on the dialogue than any other sound in your production. However, the other sounds are equally important, because they provide the mood, or ambience, of the video itself. A strong soundtrack helps viewers get into the production and have a personal experience that makes your video memorable, so let's turn our attention now to making soundtracks in Soundtrack Pro.

In this chapter you will explore techniques for spotting, or placing, sound effects at specific points in the Timeline. Along the way you'll also learn some important file-management techniques, a couple of ways to create fades, and a few other tips and tricks that will speed up your editing workflow.

The techniques you'll learn in this lesson can also be useful to Logic users who are spotting a large number of sound effects for a video project. Some users find that for video projects, Soundtrack's spotting features are more precise and flexible than Logic Pro's.

Setting Up for Spotting

We are moving on to some new source material, so take a moment to look around and familiarize yourself with the content.

1   From the source material that came with this book, open the **07 Begin.fcp** file in Final Cut Pro.

    A sequence opens in Final Cut Pro.

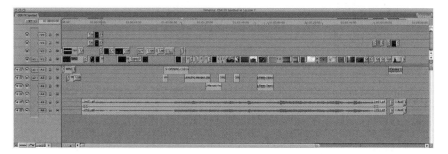

2   Play the sequence and watch the action in the Canvas window while listening carefully to the included sound effects.

    TIP If the audio clips in your Final Cut Pro sequence do not display waveforms, click the Track Layout pop-up menu (located to the right of the Timeline's Track Height controls), and choose Show Audio Waveforms.

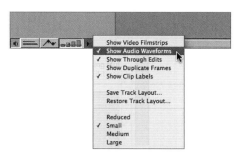

The audio in this sequence is roughed-in, and some of the effects have already been placed where they need to go in the finished sequence.

However, there's still a lot of work to do. So let's send the sequence to Soundtrack Pro for further refinement.

3 In the Browser, Control-click the *OSR FX Spotted* sequence and choose Send To > Soundtrack Pro Multitrack Project from the shortcut menu.

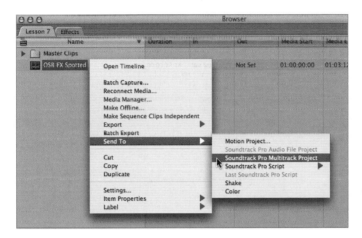

A Save dialog appears.

4   Save the new Soundtrack Pro project to a place where you can easily find
and delete it later.

NOTE ▶ The choice of where you save the project is up to you. Remember,
you've already explored the process of sending projects to Soundtrack Pro,
so we're not going to go over this dialog in detail. If you need further
instructions, please refer to the section titled "Opening a Multitrack
Project" in Lesson 4.

The project opens in Soundtrack Pro.

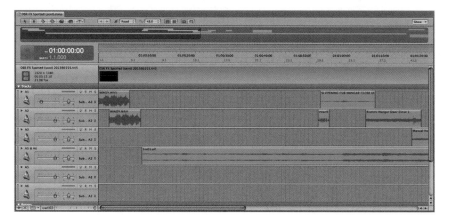

5   To ensure you can see the entire project at a glance, press Shift-Z to
zoom out.

Soundtrack Pro resizes the Timeline display so that all of the audio clips
are visible.

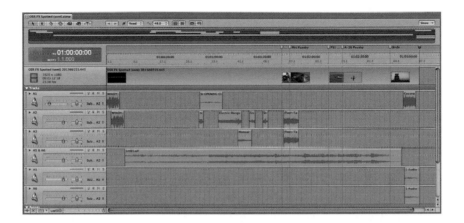

Exploring the Bin and the Browser

In Soundtrack Pro, the Bin is your project's library. You can find references to all of your project's media files here, along with important information about those files, including the sample rate, channel configuration, and even the timecode position of the file inside the project.

Opening the Bin

The Bin is located in Soundtrack Pro's lower pane. Open that pane now and take a look.

1   On the Toolbar, click the Lower Pane button.

The lower pane opens.

2   Click the Bin tab.

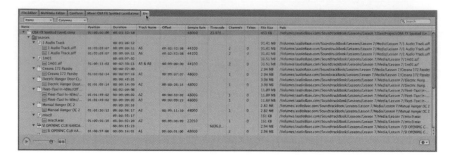

As you can see, the Bin is like a small database showing you important information about the files in your project. From file size to file location, it's all listed here.

Previewing Files in the Bin

A video score can include dozens or sometimes even hundreds of files, so you'll be forgiven if from time to time you forget which files are which as you're editing. When this happens, use the Bin's Play button to audition files so you know which file contains which sound.

1   At the lower-left corner of the Bin, set the volume slider to approximately −10 dB (50 percent).

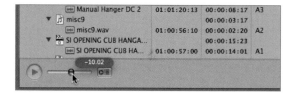

Files play automatically when they're selected in the Bin, so lowering the volume before selecting a file ensures you don't get any surprises.

2   In the Bin, select the **Cessna 172 Passby** file.

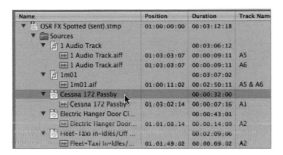

The file plays, and you hear the sound of a plane flying by.

NOTE ▶ To pause and resume playback, click the Play button located to the left of the Bin's volume slider.

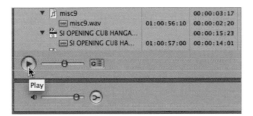

Opening the Browser

The Browser provides a quick method for you to locate files on your hard disk that you would like to add to your project. Similar to the Finder, it can be used to navigate through the folders on your computer. By default, the Browser is located on the right pane, so let's make sure that pane is open now.

1   If the right pane is not currently displayed, click the Right Pane button on the Toolbar.

The right pane opens.

2 In the lower portion of the right pane, click the Browser tab.

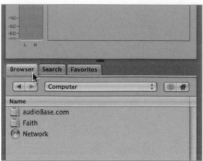

Locating Files in the Browser

At the highest level, the Browser shows you the disks mounted on your system. You can click through the disks to explore the folder hierarchy and find files you are interested in adding to your project.

1 Using the Browser, double-click through the file hierarchy on your hard disk to find the file named **SI HAND PROPPING CUB-a.mov** in the Lesson 7 folder's Media subfolder.

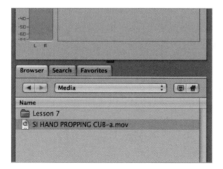

NOTE ▶ If you navigate to the wrong folder, use the navigation buttons in the upper-left corner of the Browser tab to back your way up the folder hierarchy, or use the menu located at the top of the Browser tab to jump up several folders quickly.

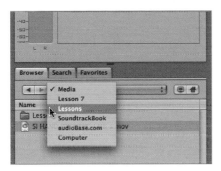

2   Click the Play button at the bottom of the Browser to audition the file and
    get a feel for the audio it contains.

Adding Browser Files to Your Project

Once you've located a file in the Browser, you can simply drag it to the Timeline.
To make it easier for you to spot this effect, some markers were added to the
project in Final Cut Pro, and those markers remained a part of the project after
you sent it to Soundtrack Pro. You'll spot this sound effect close to the first
marker (labeled *Hand Propping*).

1   From the Browser, drag the file to track A1 so it straddles the first marker.

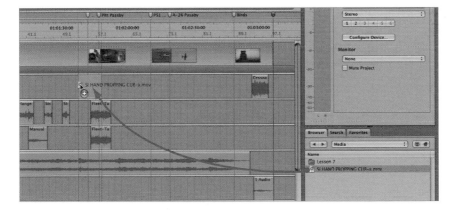

Don't worry about the exact position now. In the next section, you are
going to explore one of coolest new tools in Soundtrack Pro 2, the

Multipoint Video HUD. This heads-up display makes it easier than ever before to spot effects, so let's move on and learn more about spotting sound.

NOTE ▶ You can also drag files directly from Finder windows to your Timeline to add them to your project.

Using the Multipoint Video HUD

The Multipoint Video HUD is one of the hottest tools to be added to Soundtrack Pro 2. Spotting sound effects is an exercise in precision place-ment, and it's important to have tools that let you see clearly where you are placing your sounds. With the Multipoint Video HUD, it's a snap to spot sounds to particular frames in your project. Let's open this HUD now and take a look around.

1   Choose Window > HUDs > Multipoint Video, or press V on your keyboard.

NOTE ▶ Pressing V actually toggles the Multipoint Video HUD display, so if the HUD is not onscreen, it appears. But if the Multipoint Video HUD is onscreen when you press V, the HUD disappears.

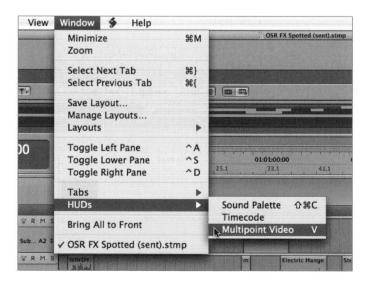

The Multipoint Video HUD opens.

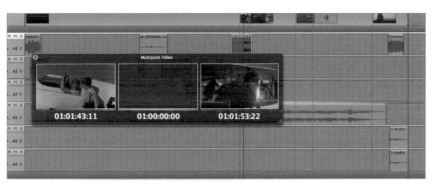

Notice the three display areas in this HUD. We'll get into what, exactly, these three areas do in a moment. For now, let's make this HUD bigger so that we can clearly see the action.

2   Drag the lower-right corner of the Multipoint Video HUD to make it bigger.

Spotting with the Multipoint Video HUD

As you saw above, the Multipoint Video HUD displays several frames of your video, each with a timecode value. This HUD's primary purpose is to provide context as you edit in Soundtrack Pro so that you can clearly see how your audio clips will line up with the video you are scoring.

This HUD behaves in different ways, depending on what you have selected in the workspace. For example, if you select a marker (with no duration) at the top of the Timeline, the Multipoint Video HUD shows only a single frame of video, because markers with no assigned duration represent only a single moment in time and are attached to one frame of video. (You'll learn more about markers and marker durations in Lesson 8.)

Single marker displayed in the Multipoint Video HUD

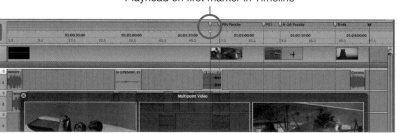

On the other hand, when you select a clip that has a duration, the left frame of the HUD shows the frame of video on the left edge of the clip, while the right frame of the HUD shows the frame of video on the right edge of the clip. However, it's the frame in the middle of the HUD that provides the magic, as it displays the frame of video directly under the pointer's position when you select the audio clip. Let's zoom in on the clip you've added to the Timeline and look at how this works.

1   Press Shift-M to move the playhead to the first marker in the Timeline (or Option-M if the playhead is after the first marker in the Timeline).

Playhead on first marker in Timeline

2   Press Command-= (equal sign) to zoom in until you can clearly see the audio clip added in the last section.

NOTE ▶ When you press Command-= to zoom in, or Command--(hyphen) to zoom out, Soundtrack Pro zooms with the playhead in the center of focus. Always remember these key commands when zooming in the Timeline.

Now that you've zoomed in on the clip, you can clearly see that there is a large section of silence at the beginning of the clip. The sound itself does not begin until the last third of the clip.

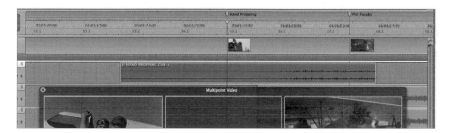

3   Position the pointer over the part of the clip where the sound begins, then click and hold.

A thin blue line extends vertically across the Timeline from the pointer's position. This line lets you visually reference the clicked point in the audio clip to the Time ruler as well as to other clips in the project. But even more important, the middle frame of the HUD updates to show you the frame of video directly under the point where you clicked.

4   Drag the clip left or right until the clicked point of the clip lines up with the first marker in the project.

Release the clip exactly on the frame where you see the actor begin pulling down on the propeller. For reference, you can see the timecode position directly under the display areas of the Multipoint Video HUD, so drop the clip when the pointer is at approximately 01:01:47:19.

5   Move the playhead to a point before the clip, and play the sequence to see (and hear) how well you've spotted this sound effect.

If you spotted the effect to the marker, it should sound pretty good. Of course, you can always use what you've learned above to refine your edit and make it perfect.

TIP To nudge clips one frame at a time, press Command–Option–Left Arrow, or Command–Option–Right Arrow.

Three-Point Edits

In the world of video editing, three-point edits provide a common technique for adding selections of larger clips to a Timeline. In a three-point edit, you specify an In point and an Out point in a long clip, and then add the selected section between the In and Out points to the Timeline at the playhead's current position.

If you are familiar with the three-point editing workflow in Final Cut Pro, you'll be happy to know that Soundtrack Pro contains a similar technique. The only major difference is that instead of editing your In and Out points in Final Cut Pro's Viewer, you edit them in Soundtrack Pro's File Editor. But other than that, the process is the same.

In the steps below, you'll use the three-point editing technique to isolate the sound of a plane zooming past the screen, and then spot the effect to a section of the Timeline that shows a plane racing past the camera.

1   In the lower pane, click the File Editor tab.

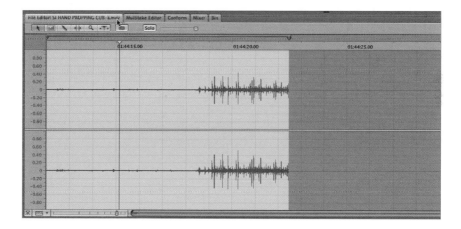

2   From the Browser, drag the **16R P51 two fly bys** file into the File Editor.

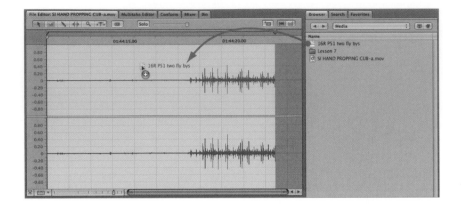

3   Press the spacebar to play the file.

As you can hear, this is a long audio file, so you should choose a smaller section of sound close to the front of the file and then add it to the project.

4   In the File Editor, make sure that the Selection tool is selected, and then drag a section of the file that encompasses approximately 10 seconds to 40 seconds from the beginning.

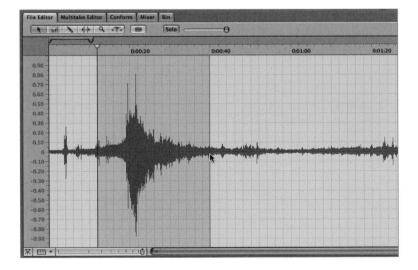

5   Press the spacebar to play the sound.

It's a plane flying by. Next, we'll spot that to the project Timeline. To make the edit easier, a marker called *P51 Fly By* has already been added to the Timeline. Move the playhead to that marker now.

6   In the Multitrack Editor, move the playhead to the *P51 Fly By* marker.

How you move the playhead is up to you. You can either click the Time ruler with the pointer at the marker's position, or press Shift-M to jump the playhead to the next marker, or use any other technique you like.

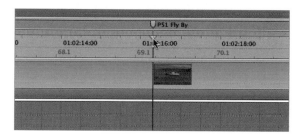

In a moment, you'll use a special feature to automatically add your audio selection from the File Editor to the Timeline in the Multitrack Editor. But before this happens, you need to tell Soundtrack Pro which track you want to add the selection to.

7   In the Multitrack Editor, select the A2 track header.

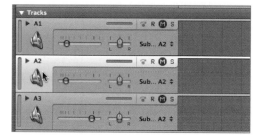

8 In the upper-right corner of the File Editor, click the Spot to Playhead button, or press Command-\ (backslash).

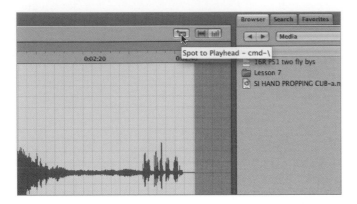

The selected part of the audio file is added to track A2 as a clip, with the left edge of the selection beginning at the playhead's position in the Timeline.

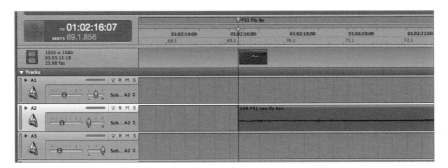

9 Play the project from slightly before the newly added clip, and listen to the effect.

Using Fades

Fades let you quickly blend clips either with silence, in the case of a fade-in or fade-out, or with other clips, in the case of a crossfade. In either situation, Soundtrack Pro provides easy techniques for working with fades. The clip you added in the steps above needs a fade-in and fade-out to smooth its entrance and exit in the project. Here's how you can add some fades.

1   Position the pointer over the upper-left corner of the **16R P51 two fly bys** clip.

    The pointer becomes a Fade pointer.

    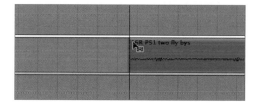

2   Drag the pointer to the right and release the mouse.

    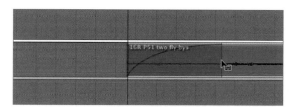

    A fade-in is created.

3   Scroll to the end of the clip and place the Fade pointer over the upper-right corner.

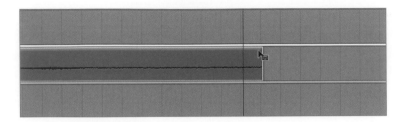

4 Drag to the left to create a fade-out.

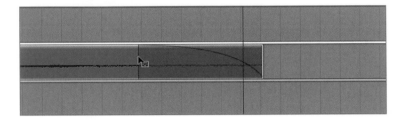

5 Play the fade and listen to the effect.

Refining Fade Duration

As you work through your project, from time to time you will need to refine your fades to make them longer or shorter. Here's how you do it.

1 Position the pointer over the left edge of the fade-out.

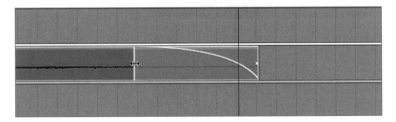

Drag handles appear on the edge of the fade and the pointer turns into a Resize pointer.

2 Drag left or right to adjust the duration of the fade.

Choosing Fade Types

Soundtrack Pro gives you access to four types of fades: one linear fade, one that increases the gain by 3 dB at the center point of the fade, one that decreases the gain by 3 dB at the center point of the fade, and one S-curve fade. To choose a fade type, follow the steps below.

1   Double-click the fade-out.

The Fade Selector appears.

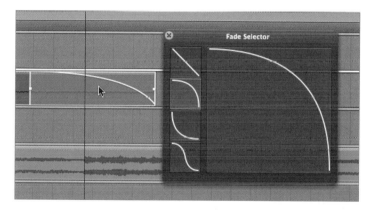

2   Click one of the fade types on the left edge of the Fade Selector.

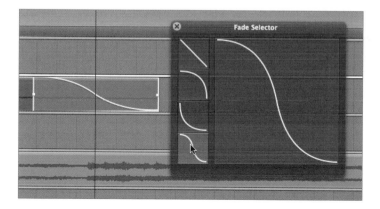

Using Envelopes to Create Fades

In the steps above, you used fades to quickly increase and decrease the volume of clips in the Timeline. While that works a treat for most situations, there will be times when you'll need more volume control than simple fades will allow. In these situations, envelopes come to the rescue.

Envelopes provide a form of automation that allows you to change volume, pan position, and several other song attributes in complex and evolving ways. If you work with Final Cut Pro, you've used envelopes before, except in Final Cut Pro the process is called keyframing. Regardless of the name, the process remains the same. In this section, you'll learn how to set envelope points by hand to create a simple fade-out, though you can apply what you learn here to all other envelopes in Soundtrack Pro, because they all work in the exact same way.

Enabling Envelopes

By default, envelopes are not enabled in Soundtrack Pro. You must turn envelopes on before you will be able to edit them. However, don't be fooled; hidden envelopes are still read by Soundtrack Pro even if you can't see them.

1   Scroll to the **SI HAND PROPPING CUB-a** clip in track A1 of the Timeline.

This clip enters with silence, so no fade-in is required. However, it exits quite suddenly, so you'll need to use the track's envelopes to add a fade-out.

2 On the A1 track, Control-click the track header and choose Show Selected Track Envelopes from the shortcut menu that appears.

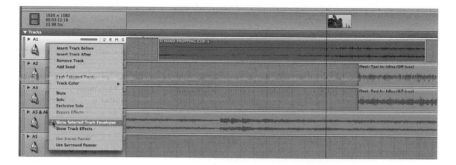

Volume and pan track envelopes appear at the bottom of the A1 track.

Creating Points

A fade-out lowers the volume until the clip can no longer be heard, so the volume envelope is a good tool to use to create a fade-out. To do this, you will create points on the envelope, and then adjust them to make a fade-out.

1 Double-click the volume envelope halfway through the "sound" portion of the clip.

An envelope point is created where you double-clicked.

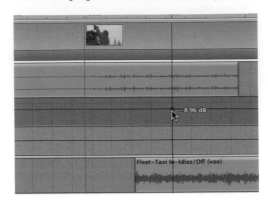

2   Double-click the volume envelope at the end of the clip.

A second envelope point is created.

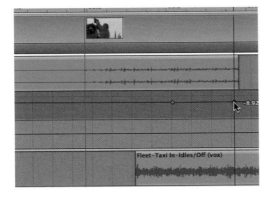

NOTE ▶ To delete an envelope point, click to select the point, and press the Delete key on your keyboard.

Adjusting Envelope Points

Now that you've created two envelope points, adjust the position of the second point to create a fade-out. Here's how.

1   Click the second point on the volume envelope, and drag down to the bottom of the automation row.

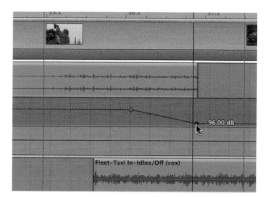

A linear fade-out is created. While this was a fairly simple example of how to use volume envelopes, it is nonetheless important for you to know this feature exists. When you need to create complex volume curves, envelopes are the only way to go. Indeed, if you scroll through the A1 track, you'll see that volume envelope points have been added to several parts of the track to adjust the volume in ways that fades alone would not allow.

Moving Envelope Points with Clips

The process of making a soundtrack is one that takes constant refinement. If you ever need to move a clip that sits over some envelope points in its track, you will need to decide whether the envelope points move with the clip or remain behind in the track.

In the case of the volume envelope created above, the envelope points should always stick to the clip to maintain the integrity of your fade-out. By default,

Soundtrack Pro is set to leave the envelope points in the track, so if you move the clip, the envelope points get left behind. Let's change that now.

1   At the top of the Multitrack Editor, click the Select Envelope Points With Clips button.

2   Drag the **SI HAND PROPPING CUB-a** clip left or right to refine its position.

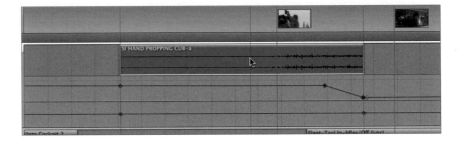

Notice that the envelope points move with the clip. Next, return Soundtrack Pro back to its default setting, which moves only the clip, and not the envelope points under it.

3   At the top of the Multitrack Editor, click the Select Only Clips button.

Lesson Review

1. What does the Bin do?

2. What does the Browser do?

3. What is the function of the Multipoint Video HUD?

4. How do you create a fade-out on a clip?

5. True or false: You cannot move envelope points at the same time as you move a clip.

Answers

1. The Bin shows you all of the media used in your project.

2. The Browser lets you search for media on your hard disk that you would like to add to the project.

3. The Multipoint Video HUD provides context for your edits by showing you the frame of video at the front of the clip in the left display area, the frame of video at the end of the clip in the right display area, and the frame of video directly under the pointer's position in the middle display area, as you move the clip, which helps you align the beginning, end, or sync point to precise video frames.

4. Position the pointer at the upper-right corner of a clip and wait until the pointer becomes a Fade pointer, and then drag to the left.

5. False: You can click the Select Envelope Points With Clips button to ensure all envelope points stick to clips when you move them.

8

Lesson Files APTS-SoundtrackPro > Lesson 08 > 08 Begin.stmp

Time This lesson takes approximately 45 minutes to complete.

Goals Set the Time ruler to Beats-based units

Explore the Search tab

Work with looping and non-looping files

Index third-party Apple Loop collections

Set the end-of-song marker

Use the Master tempo envelope

Adjust the tempo to synchronize music to specific points in your project

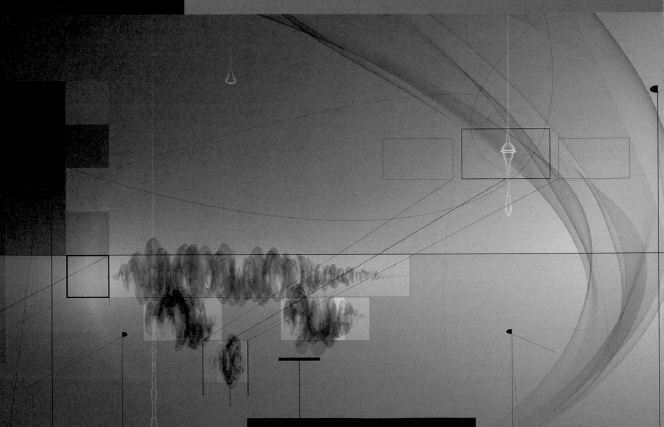

Lesson 8
Working with Musical Content

As the saying goes, "Content is king." And Soundtrack Pro is quickly becoming another monarch: the king of audio postproduction tools. For video editors, this is a great thing, because hundreds of preassembled music beds come with Soundtrack Pro, right out of the box. (A *music bed* is usually instrumental background music.) If those don't scratch your itch for great-sounding music, you can assemble your own unique soundtracks from the huge collection of Apple Loops that come with Soundtrack Pro, sample Soundtrack Pro's vast library of effects, or visit third-party sites like AudioBase.com to find unique sounds. With all this content at your disposal, you don't need to be a musician, but you do need to understand a few musical concepts so you can line up your loops to make great sound.

In this lesson you'll learn how to use Soundtrack Pro's Search tab to locate, audition, and add sounds to your project. You'll also learn some basics about how to arrange loops to create songs. In the end, you might find that making the soundtrack for your video is just as much fun as making the video itself, because designing audio with Soundtrack Pro provides oodles of instant gratification.

Setting Up for Music Production

In music, time is measured in beats and bars, while in video time is measured in hours, minutes, seconds, and frames (also known as SMPTE timecode, after the Society of Motion Picture and Television Engineers, which established the standard). By default, the Soundtrack Pro Time ruler is set to SMPTE time-code units. That's great for doing dialogue replacement or spotting effects to specific frames of video, but to make the music for your soundtrack, you need to switch to a more musical measurement system. You'll learn how to config-ure Soundtrack Pro for music production in the following steps.

Switching to the Beats-Based Ruler

With the ruler set to display timecode, the gridlines in the project align to frames in the video. On the other hand, when you set the ruler to display beats, the gridlines become a bit more musical and align to beats and bars, which is necessary for arranging loops to make a song. Let's switch the ruler units now.

1   Continue working on your project from the last chapter, or open the file titled **08 Begin.stmp** in the Lesson 08 folder.

2   In the left pane, click the Project tab.

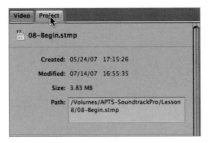

3 Scroll down the Project tab to the Properties area.

4 Set the Rule Unit menu to Beats.

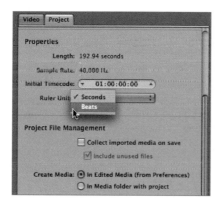

At the top of the Timeline, the ruler updates to display beats as the primary measurement unit, and the grid now aligns to music beats. For reference, you can still see the SMPTE timecode values along the bottom of the ruler.

Ruler and gridlines display bars and beats.

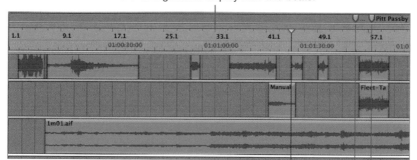

Using the Search Tab

The Search tab is your first port of call when you are looking for sounds to add to your project. If you installed the Soundtrack Pro content discs that came with Final Cut Studio, this tab will be populated with thousands of loops, music beds, and sound effects. With all this content at your disposal, the Search tab becomes a very important part of your music-making workflow.

Opening the Search Tab

The Search tab is located in the bottom section of Soundtrack Pro's right pane. Open it now and take a look around.

1 If the right pane is not showing, click the Right Pane button toward the right edge of Soundtrack Pro's Toolbar.

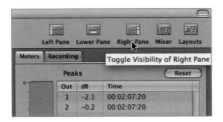

2 In the bottom section of the right pane, click the Search tab.

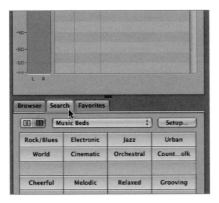

The Search tab itself is divided into three main sections. At the top are Button and Column View buttons used to quickly search broad categories and genres. In the middle is the search-refinement area, which you can use to limit your search results to audio files of a specific time signature or music key, or with names that include specific keywords. At the bottom is a Search Results list that shows you audio files that match your search terms.

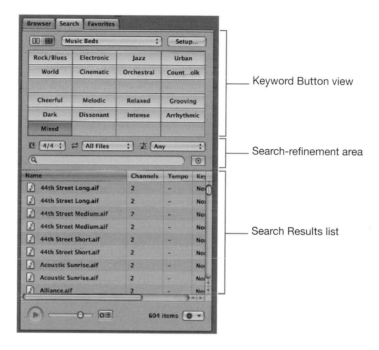

Keyword Button view

Search-refinement area

Search Results list

Looping vs. Non-looping Files

The Search tab can list both looping and non-looping files, and the difference between the two is important.

Looping files are song-construction parts you can stack and layer to make your own songs in Soundtrack Pro. Looping files are restricted to a maximum of 32 beats, and they will loop seamlessly in your Soundtrack Pro projects for as long as you need them to. Looping files usually have tempo and key information included to help you determine which files will mix together to make great-sounding music. These files also work seamlessly with Soundtrack Pro scoring markers; they contain information Soundtrack Pro can use to change their tempo without affecting their pitch (the way they sound), as you'll learn later in this lesson.

Non-looping files are sound effects or music beds that can be longer than 32 beats. Non-looping files rarely have tempo or key information and are not meant to be layered with other files to create music (with the possible exception of some audio effects files). For example, the music beds that come with Soundtrack Pro are entire songs in their own right, so all you need to do is find a song that reflects the mood you are after and add it to your project. One thing to note is that because non-looping files do not contain tempo information, they will not automatically time stretch as you change tempo in your project.

Let's begin by looking at non-looping files and, specifically, music beds.

1 In the center portion of the Search tab, set the File Type pop-up menu to Non-looping.

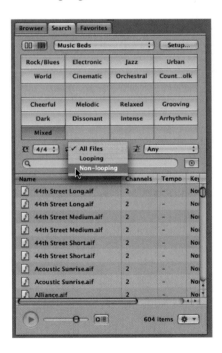

2   At the top of the Search tab, set the Category pop-up menu to Music Beds.

In the Search Results list, only non-looping music beds are displayed.

Button View vs. Column View

The Search tab's main strength is its ability to let you quickly home in on specific types of music by clicking keyword categories. To this end, the Search tab contains two views: the Button and Column views. Each view contains slightly different options, so to get a feel for each, toggle the display of these views using the steps below and determine which view you prefer to work with.

1   In the upper-left corner of the Search tab, click the Column View button.

The top area of the Search tab splits into two columns, one for keywords and one for matches.

2   Scroll down the list of keywords and check out what's on offer.

As you'll come to see, a lot more keywords are listed in Column view than in Button view. This can make it easier to find files of a certain type, particularly when it comes to instrument loops and sound effects.

3   In the upper-left corner of the Search tab, click the Button View button.

The top area of the Search tab shows keyword buttons labeled with genres of music. Although fewer choices are listed in the Button view than in the Column view, the Button view has a bonus: You can click multiple keyword buttons to expand your search to loops in two or more genres.

4   Click two or more keyword buttons.

NOTE ▶ To deselect a keyword button, click it again.

Auditioning Loops

When you click files in the Search Results list, they automatically play, and if the files are loops, they even play at the same tempo as your project, but more on that later in this lesson. For now, let's adjust the volume so no speakers are harmed during the next steps, and then listen to some music beds.

1   At the bottom of the Search tab, drag the volume slider to approximately halfway.

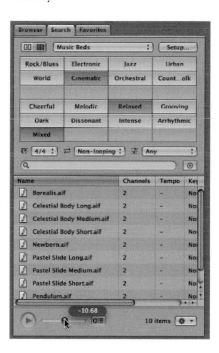

2   In the Search Results list, click a file to audition it.

The file is highlighted and begins playing.

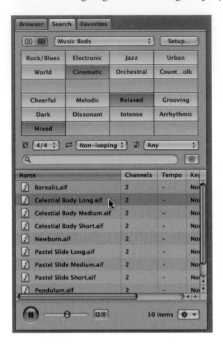

3   To stop playback, click the Pause button in the lower-left corner of the Search tab.

NOTE ▶ After selecting a file in the Results list, use the arrow keys to move up or down the list to audition more files.

Adding Music Beds

The project you are working on includes some background audio. This audio was supplied by the director to give you a feel for the type of score that should be used in the finished project, and it's anyone's guess if the music is royalty free or not. But that does not matter, because in a second you will remove that audio and replace it with some music beds from the discs that came with Soundtrack Pro. All of the content on these discs is royalty free, so you can use it in any production you choose without worrying about getting a nasty letter from a copyright lawyer.

> **NOTE ▶** If you have not already installed the content discs that came with Final Cut Studio, please do so now. You'll need this content to follow along with the next steps.

Let's remove the project's current music bed and replace it with some music beds from Soundtrack Pro.

1   Select the clip in track A5 & A6.

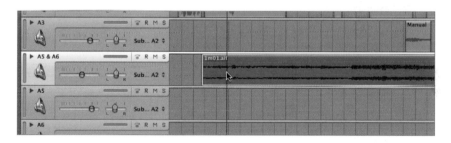

2   Press the Delete key.

The clip is deleted.

Searching by Keyword

While the Column and Button views go a long way toward helping you locate loops, nothing beats searching by an *actual* keyword, especially if you already know what loops you are interested in. For example, the content that comes with Soundtrack Pro includes hundreds of music beds, and these beds all come in both long and short forms, each tagged appropriately with either *long* or *short* appended to the filename. There's several minutes of space to fill in this project, so you'll need to refine your search to find only the loops with *long* in their names.

1   In the Button view at the top of the Search tab, make sure that no buttons are selected.

When you enter a keyword search, Soundtrack Pro searches only the files that are tagged with the genres you select in the Button view. Deselect all genres now to conduct the broadest search possible.

2   Halfway down the Search tab, type the word *long* into the Search field.

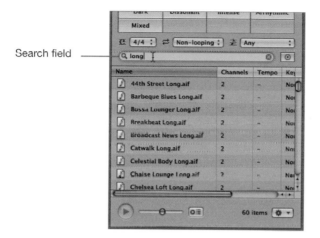

Search field

Only files with the word *long* in their names are listed in the Search Results list.

3　Audition several of the result files to get a feel for the types of music they contain.

NOTE ▶ To find out the duration of a loop, Control-click it in the Search Results list and choose "Reveal in Finder" from the shortcut menu. This will pop open a Finder window, and the loop will be automatically selected. If you look at the loop in the Finder's column view (Command-3), you'll see the duration of the loop listed there.

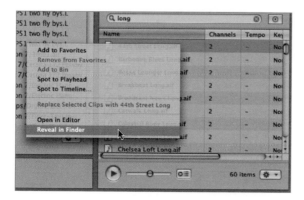

Spotting Files to the Timeline

Intuitively, you can just drag files from the Search tab to the Timeline to insert them into your project. However, sometimes that method does not provide the most exact placement of the sounds into your Timeline, so let's look at a more advanced option: spotting sounds from the Search tab into set tracks.

1   In the upper-left corner of the Multitrack Editor, double-click the Beats display.

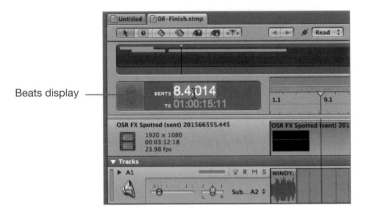

Beats display

A text entry field appears.

2   Type the number *7* and press Return.

NOTE ▸ Remember, earlier in this lesson you switched the Time ruler to measure in beats, so the playhead jumps to the beginning of bar 7. Note that you don't have to type in the exact beat coordinate, because Soundtrack Pro is able to make certain assumptions for you. For example, if you type in only a single number, Soundtrack Pro assumes you want to jump to the beginning of a bar. If, on the other hand, you were to type in the number 7.2, Soundtrack Pro would jump to bar 7, beat 2. Isn't that handy?

3   Make sure that the A5 & A6 track is selected in the Timeline.

In the next step, Soundtrack Pro will spot an audio file to the playhead's position in the currently selected track, so it's important you have the correct track selected to begin with.

4   In the Search tab, Control-click the **44th Street Long.aif** loop, and choose "Spot to Playhead" from the shortcut menu (or if you've found a different music bed you like, feel free to spot that file to the playhead).

Soundtrack Pro adds the file to the Timeline at the playhead's position in the currently selected track.

Using Crossfades

The music bed you added probably doesn't fill the Timeline, which means you'll need to import additional music beds into the project. Soundtrack Pro makes that easy to do by providing a dedicated crossfade mode.

In Lesson 5, you learned about Soundtrack Pro's truncate mode. Specifically, you saw that truncate mode causes the deletion of any part of a clip that is overlapped by another clip. When you use crossfade mode, Soundtrack Pro seamlessly crossfades from one clip to the next, creating a smooth transition. Let's explore crossfade mode in further detail now.

1   At the top of the Multitrack Editor, click the Crossfade Mode button.

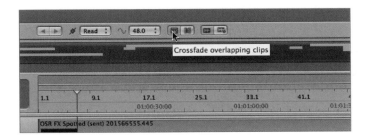

2   In the Search tab, find a music bed file that you like (you are the audio engineer here, so the choice is yours).

3   Drag the file from the Search Results list, and drop it over the tail of the **44th Street Long.aif** audio clip in the Timeline.

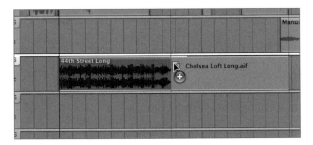

A new audio clip is added to the Timeline and a crossfade is automatically created between the overlapping clips. Note that by default, the amount of overlap determines the length of the crossfade.

Refining the Crossfade

By default, Soundtrack Pro crossfades from the beginning of the second clip to the end of the first clip—in other words, it crossfades for the entire duration of the overlap between the two clips. You can shorten the crossfade by following the steps below.

1 Position the pointer over the crossfade.

The crossfade is outlined in white, and handles appear on its left and right edges.

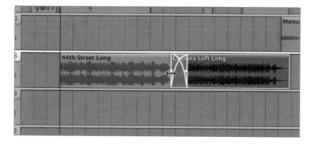

2 Drag either one of the handles to adjust the duration of the crossfade.

Working with Loops

The music beds that come with Soundtrack Pro are great for small spots such as an intro segment or a DVD-Video menu. But if your segment is longer than a minute or so, you'll probably want to create your own score using Apple Loops.

For soundtrack designers, Apple Loops provide several benefits. For starters, you can loop Apple Loops for as long as you need to fill the duration of the spot you are scoring. Apple Loops also change tempo to match the tempo of the project you are working on. You can easily layer Apple Loops to create complex arrangements and even adjust their pitch, ensuring that there's no clash of sound or key in your composition. Not only does Soundtrack Pro come with hundreds of Apple Loops, but you can also add loops from other applications such as GarageBand, purchase additional loops from Apple in the form of Jam Packs, or download loops from third-party vendors such as AudioBase.com. With all this content available, it's a good thing you have the Search tab to help you find the content you're after.

TIP ▶ You can create more diverse scores using Apple Loops with Logic Pro than you can with Soundtrack Pro. Apple Loops function nearly identically in Soundtrack Pro and Logic, with one exception: Soundtrack Pro does not support the use of MIDI Apple Loops. MIDI Apple Loops offer more flexibility—their musical performances can be extensively edited on a note by note basis and the performances can be reassigned to different instruments altogether. For information on using Apple Loops in Logic, reference *Apple Pro Training Series: Logic Pro 8 and Logic Express 8*.

Adding Third-Party Apple Loops

Uniqueness is the key to any audio production, and at some point you'll want to branch out from the loops that come with Soundtrack Pro. You can do this by purchasing Apple's Jam Packs, or downloading Apple Loops from one of the dozens of sample sites on the web. Typically, downloaded loops will come in a zipped archive, so the steps below show you how to make these loops available in Soundtrack Pro.

NOTE ▸ To jump-start you on the path to new content, use the coupon code APTS25 to save 25 percent off all Apple Loop collections at AudioBase.com.

1 In the upper-right corner of the Search tab, click the Setup button.

The Setup dialog with an indexed list drops down from Soundtrack Pro's title bar.

2 In the upper-left corner of the dialog, click the Add Directory button.

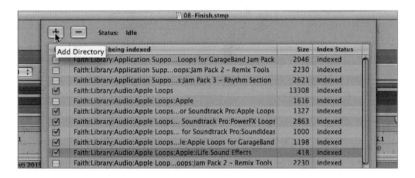

An Open dialog appears.

3 Navigate to the folder containing your third-party loops, and click the Open button.

The loops are added to the list in the Setup dialog. However, the Search tab won't display them yet. In fact, if you look closely you'll see that the newly added Apple Loop collection is not indexed. Soundtrack Pro must first analyze, or index, the Apple Loops and add them to its registry of audio content available for your projects.

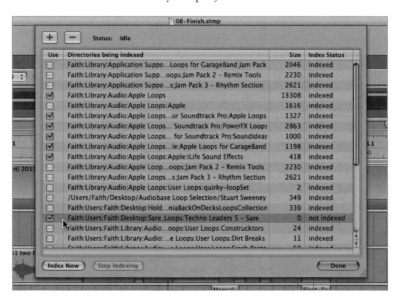

4   In the lower-left corner of the dialog, click the Index Now button.

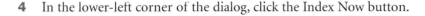
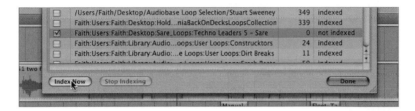

A status display appears at the top of the dialog so you can follow along as Soundtrack Pro indexes your new Apple Loops.

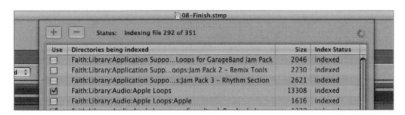

Once the loops are indexed, you can locate them using Soundtrack Pro's Search tab.

5   In the dialog, click the Done button.

The indexed list closes.

Adding Apple Loops to Your Project

In general, you add Apple Loops to your project in the same way you'd add any other audio file from the Search tab. However, before searching for Apple Loops, make sure that the Search tab's File Type pop-up menu is set to Looping, or you won't find any usable content. Then search for loops by genre, and select any loop you feel represents the mood of the music you want in your project. Music is a highly subjective pastime, so express your creativity by searching for and adding whatever loops you want to the project. The following steps serve as a guide.

1   In the Search tab, set the File Type pop-up menu to Looping.

2   Mute the track that contains the music beds you added in the previous
    section of this lesson.

With the old music beds muted, it's time to create a new track to hold
some Apple Loops.

3   Control-click the track header to create a new track directly under the
    muted track in the Timeline.

4   Use the techniques you learned earlier in this lesson to search for an Apple
    Loop you would like to add to the project.

5   Drag the Apple Loop from the Browser, and drop it onto the A5 track at
     bar 7 of the Timeline.

     NOTE ▶ If snapping is turned off, press the Command key as you drag
     the loop into the project. Pressing the Command key as you drag audio
     files into Soundtrack Pro temporarily toggles the snapping mode, so if
     snapping is off it will be temporarily enabled. This in turn ensures that
     you will drop the new file exactly on bar and beat.

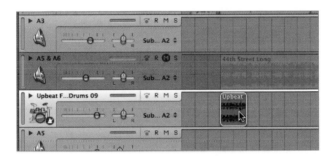

Looping Apple Loops

As the name implies, Apple Loops are meant to loop, or repeat, seamlessly, for
as long as you need them to do so. Fortunately, Soundtrack Pro makes this
process as simple as a quick click and drag.

1   Position the pointer over the right edge of the newly added Apple Loop.

     The pointer becomes a Clip Resize pointer.

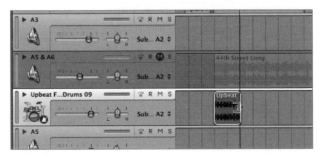

2   Drag the Clip Resize pointer to the right.

As you drag, Soundtrack Pro automatically loops the audio clip.

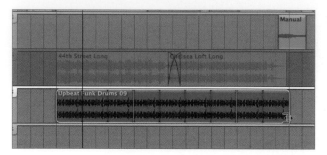

And that's about all there is to it. Now, building your soundtrack is as simple as adding more tracks and loops to your project. But there is one more thing. . .

Setting the Tempo

The best thing about Apple Loops is that they automatically adjust to match the tempo of your project. This is an awesome feature, because it makes it extremely easy to mix and match loops of different tempos to make music that almost always sounds good. Admittedly, you don't want to stray too far from the original tempo of the loop—any deviation of more than 20 percent from the loop's original tempo will create noticeable artifacts in the sound. With this one provision, feel free to experiment, mixing different styles of loops together in new and interesting musical creations.

With this in mind, change the tempo of the song to see how it affects the playback of your newly added Apple Loop(s).

1   In the ruler at the top of the Timeline, drag from left to right to set a cycle region from bar 9 to bar 25.

That's an 8-bar loop. By setting the song to cycle, you can listen along and hear the tempo changes you'll make in the steps below.

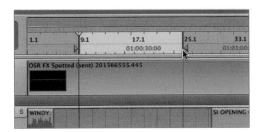

2   Press the spacebar to play the cycle region.

3   On the left pane's Project tab, scroll down to the Music section, located at the very bottom of the tab.

The Tempo value slider is here.

4   Click the value in the value slider, then drag the slider left or right to change the project's tempo.

5   Set the tempo to 104 BPM.

NOTE ▶ This setting will become important to ensure you can successfully follow the steps later in this project.

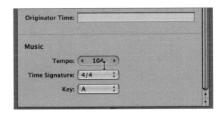

NOTE ▶ You can also double-click the Tempo value and type in a value.

As you change the tempo, notice that Soundtrack Pro adjusts the playback speed of your Apple Loop(s). Now that's audio production power!

At this point, feel free to play a bit by adding more tracks and Apple Loops until you've created an arrangement you like, then continue to the final section of this lesson.

Using Markers

Markers sit above the Time ruler and are primarily used to identify sections of your song. For example, you can use markers to identify a frame of video to spot a sound effect, or the beginning of a musical chorus. But there are other important uses for markers, so let's explore a few.

Setting the End-of-Song Marker

In Soundtrack Pro, normal markers are green, but a red marker denotes the end of the song or project. This marker is used by Soundtrack Pro to determine where to stop when it comes time to bounce out your song ("bouncing" is the process of rendering a final audio file for import into Final Cut Pro, recording to an audio CD, etc.). Typically, you will set the end-of-song marker to the last frame of video (or the end of the final audio clip) in your project, though you can move it forward if you want to bounce an earlier section of the song.

> **NOTE ▶** If you have a cycle region defined in the ruler, Soundtrack Pro will bounce only the section of the song contained within the cycle region.

In the project you are working on, Soundtrack Pro automatically inserted an end-of-song marker when the project was sent from Final Cut Pro. But this isn't always the case. In fact, when you create a new multitrack project, there is no end-of-song marker and it's up to you to create one. Let's look at the process now.

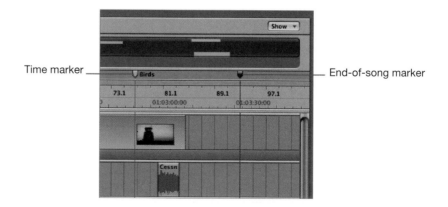

Time marker ————   ———— End-of-song marker

1   Click the end-of-song marker to select it.

2   Press the Delete key.

Soundtrack Pro deletes the end-of-song marker.

3   Position the playhead at the end of the video clip.

NOTE ▶ If snapping is not enabled, press the Command key while positioning the playhead. This will force the playhead to snap to the end of the video clip.

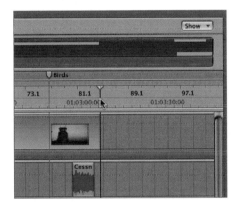

4   Choose Mark > Set End of Project.

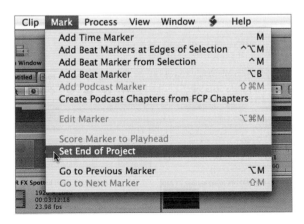

An end-of-song marker is created at the playhead's current position in the Timeline, which conveniently happens to be the end of the song.

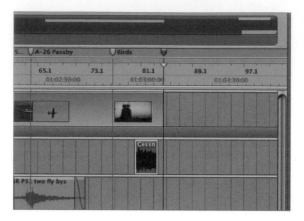

NOTE ▶ If you are using reverbs, delays, or other effects that cause a gradual trailing off of the sounds in the music portion of the project, you may want to set the end-of-song marker to a few frames after the end of the project so the reverb "tails" won't get cut off when you export the project. Of course, this also means that the exported audio file will be longer than the corresponding video clip once you bring the audio file back into Final Cut Pro. Consequently, you may have to do some planning to ensure that your audio stops before the video, which in turn will ensure that all reverb tails remain within the duration of the video clip.

Adding Markers to the Timeline

The end-of-song marker is static and has one purpose: to signify the end of the song when your project is exported. Soundtrack Pro also contains two other types of markers, *time* and *beat*. You can tell these two markers apart in the Timeline because time markers are green, while beat markers are purple. Let's add one of each to the project.

1 Move the playhead to bar 26, beat 1.

2   Press the M key on your keyboard.

NOTE ▶ This step assumes you are using a tempo of 104 BPM, as set a few sections ago.

A green time marker is set in the Timeline. Bar 26 roughly syncs to a point where the scene changes from the intro to a man opening a sliding hangar door. In the following scene, you'll take a nostalgic journey through the history of aviation, so it's a good place to drop a marker.

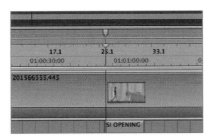

3   Move the playhead to the beginning of bar 54.

4   Press Option-B.

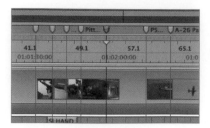

A purple beat marker is created. This point in the project signifies the end of the nostalgic scene and the transition into present-day aviation. In a moment, you'll use the markers set above to dramatically change the tempo of your project, but more on that later. For now, you'll learn a bit more about marker properties.

Naming Markers

Providing descriptive names for your markers is always a good idea. It helps to jog your memory and remind you what section of music lies under the marker, and you can even use them to jot down quick notes for later reference.

1   Select the time marker you inserted at the beginning of bar 26.

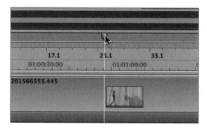

2   On the left pane, click the Details tab.

With the marker selected in the Timeline, the Details tab shows you information about the marker.

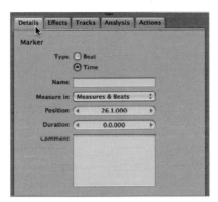

3   In the Details tab's Name field, type *Scene 2*.

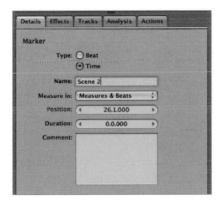

In the Timeline, the words *Scene 2* have been appended to the marker.

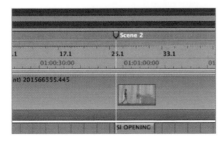

Adjusting Marker Duration

One of the coolest features of markers is their ability to represent duration in the Timeline. This is a great way to denote individual scenes in the video, or music phrases in your scores.

1   In the Details tab, double-click the number in Duration value slider.

2   Enter *28* (for 28 bars) as the Duration value.

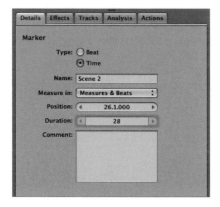

Back in the Timeline, notice that a bar now extends from the marker, and all of Scene 2 is now visually highlighted.

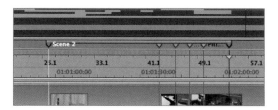

NOTE ► If you've defined a marker duration, you can quickly create a cycle region the same length as the marker duration by Control-clicking the marker and choosing "Create Cycle Region from Marker."

Using Markers to Set Tempo

Now it's time to do something really cool with markers. As you score your videos, there will be times when you want a certain section of music to fit snugly between two separate sync points in the video. For example, you might have a section of soundtrack that should be heard *only* during a particular scene. If you've designed a soundtrack using Apple Loops, you can easily do this. Essentially, Soundtrack Pro will automatically adjust the tempo of the section you specify so that the music exactly fills the required space.

This is a bit of an advanced technique, so make sure you follow the steps below closely. Also, please note this technique works only with looping Apple Loops. If your sequence contains non-looping files, you won't get the results you expect. With those two provisions in mind, open up the master tempo envelope and begin.

Using the Master Tempo Envelope

Master envelopes are a form of automation used to control the volume, transpose value, and tempo of your song. These are similar to the volume envelopes discussed in Lesson 7, except instead of affecting just a single track, they affect all tracks in your project, simultaneously. Let's enable the Master tempo envelope now.

1   In the Multitrack Editor, scroll to the very bottom.

The Master bus becomes visible directly under the Submixes area.

2   If the Master bus area is closed, click the disclosure triangle to open it.

The Master bus area opens to reveal a volume envelope.

3   From the Show Envelopes menu, choose Tempo.

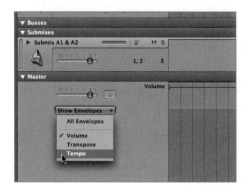

The tempo envelope is revealed.

4   Click the first envelope point at the beginning of the tempo envelope.

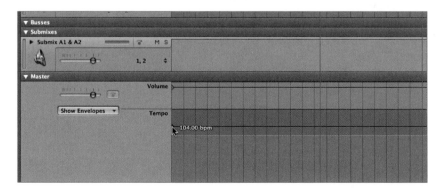

The project's tempo is displayed.

Scoring Tempo Changes

In the steps below, you will adjust the project tempo for only a certain section of the score. Specifically, you will ensure that a specified section of your Apple Loop soundtrack will fit snugly between the markers you created above.

1 At the Scene 2 marker, double-click the tempo envelope to create an envelope point.

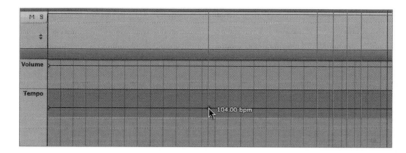

This point will be used to signify the beginning of the tempo change.

2 Position the playhead at bar 39.

The position of the playhead indicates the end point in your Apple Loop soundtrack that you want to sync. We've chosen a somewhat arbitrary point for demonstration, but you can put the playhead at *any* point in the Timeline that makes sense, based on the soundtrack you've produced.

3 Select the marker directly after the playhead's position in the Timeline.

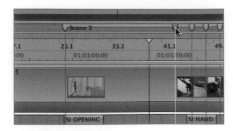

4   Choose Mark > Score Marker to Playhead.

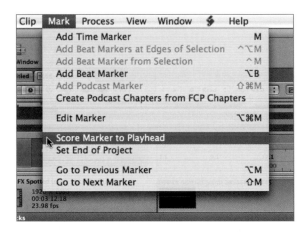

A few things happen. First, the Timeline updates and the section of Apple Loops between the tempo envelope point you inserted above and the playhead's position expands to fill the space between the first two markers in the Timeline. Second, as you modify the Master tempo envelope to reflect this new change in tempo, the tempo decreases during this section.

5   Play the song and listen to the tempo change.

As you can see (and hear), only the tracks containing Apple Loops have been affected by your tempo envelope changes. All of your non-looping audio clips, including the effects you've spotted to the Timeline, remain in their exact time positions relative to the video and have not been affected by this edit. That's a good thing, because if they were anchored to the beat grid, they would now all be out of sync with your video. Keep this trick in mind when it comes time to score your videos, because it's a great way to fit music into certain sections of your video production.

Lesson Review

1.   How do you set the Time ruler to Beats-based units?

2.   What does the Search tab do?

3.   How do you loop Apple Loops in the Timeline?

4.   True or false: Once you set a crossfade, you cannot change its duration.

5.   What does the end-of-song marker do?

Answers

1.   Visit the Project tab's Properties area, and set the Ruler Unit menu to Beats.

2.   The Search tab lets you quickly locate and audition indexed Apple Loops, music beds, and audio effects files on your hard disk.

3.   Drag the right edge of the Apple Loop audio clip, and Soundtrack Pro will automatically loop the clip as many times as you need.

4.   False: You can adjust the duration of a crossfade by dragging its edges to resize it.

5.   The end-of-song marker indicates the duration of the track and will be used to set the area to export (as long as a cycle region is not defined in the project).

9

Lesson **9**

Mixing Multitrack Projects

Mixing is the art of balancing the sound in your project so it is pleasing and musical to the ear. This process involves simple things like adjusting the volume of tracks relative to one another and balancing the pan of certain sounds in the stereo (or surround) space. It also takes into account more complex topics such as adding equalizers to make certain frequencies more pronounced in the final "mix" and using dynamic range compression to give more presence to sounds such as vocals. Finally, advanced features such as buses and submixes all add to a polished sound. As the mix engineer, you need to understand all of these concepts to put a final sparkle on your projects.

Exploring the Mixer

The Mixer tab mimics the look of a classic hardware mixing console that you might find in a high-end audio production facility. A series of *channel strips* (one for each track in the Multitrack Editor) shows you the relationship between the volume and pan position of each track at a glance. You can also use the Mixer to mute and isolate tracks, add digital signal processing (DSP) effects, and even arm tracks for recording. Some of these concepts have been covered in previous lessons, while others (such as using DSP effects) will be covered a bit later in this lesson. In any case, it's important to understand the layout of a channel strip, so let's open the Mixer now and take a look around.

1   Open the file **09 Begin.stmp** in the Lesson 09 folder.

    If you're using the lesson file that came with this book, only the first minute of the file has been scored, to make it easier to follow along.

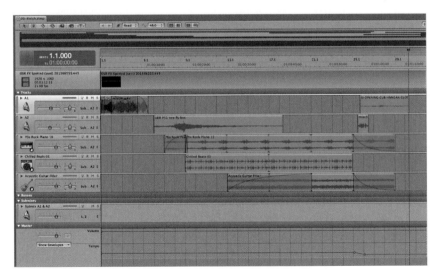

2   If the lower pane is not displayed, click the Lower Pane button in the upper-right corner of the Toolbar.

3   In the Toolbar, click the Mixer button.

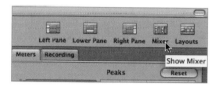

The Mixer opens in the lower pane. Take a moment to explore the Mixer carefully and orient yourself to its different sections.

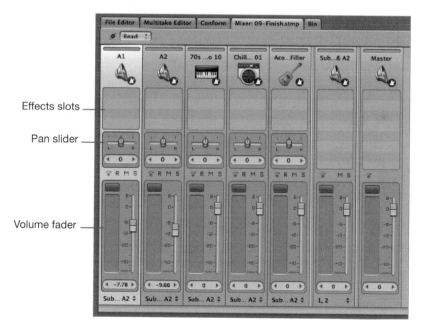

Effects slots

Pan slider

Volume fader

NOTE ▸ If your system is set up with multiple displays, choose Window > Layouts > Separate Mixer and Video. This layout pulls the Mixer and Video tabs into their own windows, which you may then arrange across your displays, making it easier to arrange and mix your project at the same time. Additionally, putting the Mixer window on its own display lets you make the channel strips taller, which in turn makes the volume slider taller, allowing you to adjust the volume in finer increments.

Adjusting Volume in the Mixer

This project has not yet been mixed. A few Apple Loops have been added to create a simple soundtrack, and some fades have been used to gradually bring in the sounds. But other than that, all of the loops are playing at their default volume. Before you get down to the serious business of mixing, though, create a cycle region so that the sounds play repeatedly, which will give you a good feel for the volume levels you are adjusting.

1   Create a cycle region from bar 13 to bar 17.

2   Press the spacebar to play the cycle region.

3   As the cycle plays, adjust the volume sliders on the three Apple Loop
tracks until they sound like they are playing with proportional volume
(for example, choose settings where the drums do not overpower the
guitar and where the keyboard melody is dominant).

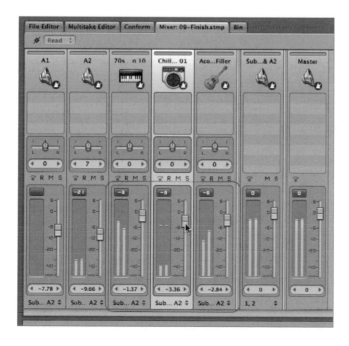

By the way, don't worry about the volume of the sound effects in tracks 1 and 2 just yet. We'll get to that later in the lesson when we discuss sub-mixes. For now, adjust only the Apple Loops tracks.

4 When you are finished adjusting the volume, press the spacebar to stop playback.

Adjusting Pan in the Mixer

The panorama potentiometer, or pan control, is used to place sounds in the stereo (or surround) spectrum. Imagine your soundtrack as a photo of a panoramic landscape: if you piled all of the trees, bushes, and lakes directly into the center of the photo, the image composition would not be very interesting. But if the trees, bushes, and lakes were spread out from left to right across the image, each in its own perfect place, then the landscape would feel balanced and be pleasing to gaze at. Similarly, the individual instruments and effects in a soundscape should be spread across the stereo image like the members of a band spread across the stage, and not piled one on top of the other in the middle of the stereo field. This is where the pan setting comes into play. Let's adjust the pan of the loops in this project to ensure the piano and guitar sounds are sitting in their own space in the stereo spectrum.

1 Press the spacebar to play the cycle region.

2 On the Piano channel strip, drag the pan slider to the left until the display area directly under it reads –55.

NOTE ▶ In Soundtrack Pro, pan can be set from –100 (full left) to 100 (full right), with 0 being directly in the middle.

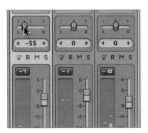

3   On the guitar track, double-click the value slider under the pan slider.

A text field appears.

4   Type *55* and press Return.

The guitar sound pans to the right, about halfway.

5   Press the spacebar to stop playback.

Using the Tracks Tab Channel Strip

The lower pane takes up a lot of screen real estate. If you're using Soundtrack Pro on a laptop, that might become an issue, because having the lower pane displayed limits the number of tracks you can see in the Multitrack Editor. Happily, Soundtrack Pro provides access to track channel strips in a second area of the interface—the Tracks tab. Let's open the Tracks tab now and take a look.

1   If the left pane is not visible, click the Left Pane button in the upper-right corner of the Toolbar.

2 In the bottom portion of the left pane, click the Tracks tab.

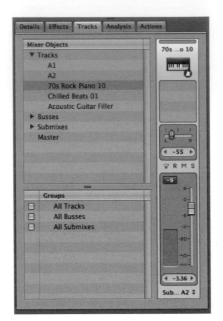

Notice there is a channel strip displayed on the right edge of the Tracks tab. This channel strip updates to display whatever track is currently selected in the Multitrack Editor or Mixer window. Let's test that theory now.

3 In the Multitrack Editor, select a new track.

NOTE ► You can also select tracks directly in the Tracks tab's Mixer Objects area and the Tracks tab channel strip will update to display the settings for the selected track.

The Tracks tab channel strip updates to show the settings for the selected track. That's a pretty cool feature of the Tracks tab, but there are some other interesting things found here as well. Let's pause in the Tracks tab for a moment and discuss submixes and, a bit later, buses.

Using Submixes

A submix is a collection of tracks controlled by a single channel strip. In Soundtrack Pro, every track is routed to a submix before exiting the application through the Master bus. Indeed, if you look closely at the Mixer tab now, you'll see both a submix channel strip and the Master channel strip on the right side of the tab. This traces the general left-to-right path of audio routing through Soundtrack Pro's Mixer—in other words, tracks route the signal to the submix, which in turn routes the signal to the Master bus.

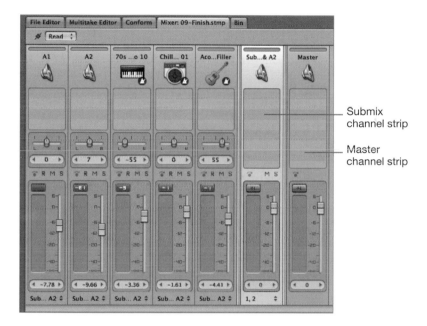

Submix channel strip

Master channel strip

The greatest virtue of a submix is that you can easily control the volume of a group of tracks using a single fader. In practice, you set the relative volume of a group of tracks by adjusting their individual volume faders to create a mix, and then use the submix to control the overall volume of all the submix tracks at one time. You can also enhance the sound of the submix by applying DSP effects directly to the submix channel itself. As you are starting to see, submixes are a powerful mixing tool!

In the project you are currently working on, there are two types of tracks. First there are effects tracks, which include some wind noise and the sound of planes zooming past the camera. Second, there are the Apple Loops that make up the simple soundtrack. Let's route each type of track to its own submix now.

1   Choose Multitrack > Add Submix (Option-Command-T).

A new submix is added to both the Tracks tab and the Mixer tab.

To route tracks to submixes, use the Submix menu at the bottom of each track's channel strip in the Mixer.

2   On the 70s Rock Piano track, click the Submix menu and choose Submix 2.

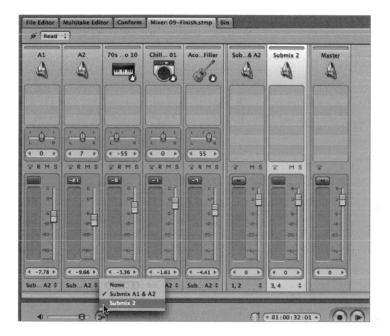

The 70s Rock Piano track is now routed to Submix 2.

3   Route the Chilled Beats and Acoustic Guitar Filler tracks to Submix 2.

Choosing Audio Interface Outputs

Each submix can be sent to different outputs on your audio interface. If you have more than two (stereo) outputs on your audio interface, you need to tell Soundtrack Pro which outputs to route the submix to. To do so, use the Output menu at the bottom of each channel strip.

> **NOTE ▶** The Master fader controls the volume of all submixes, regardless of the outputs you route the submix to.

1 From the Output menu at the bottom of the Submix 2 channel strip, choose Stereo > 1, 2.

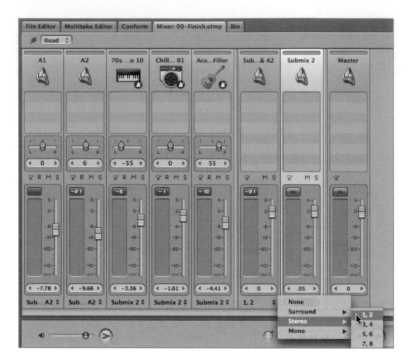

2 Play the cycle region.

3 Adjust the volume of Submix 2 and listen to the effect it has on your soundtrack.

4 Press the spacebar to stop playback.

We're done mixing this part of the track for now, so let's turn off the cycle region.

5 At the top of the Multitrack Editor, Control-click the ruler and choose Cycle Region > Remove Cycle Region (Option-X).

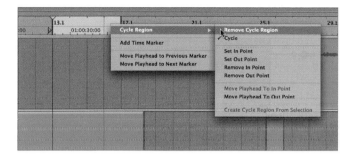

The cycle region is removed.

Naming Submixes

You should always name your submixes to reflect the types of sounds passing through them. Otherwise, it's easy to adjust the wrong submix when you get deep into mixing.

1   In the Mixer, click the name at the top of Submix A1 & A2.

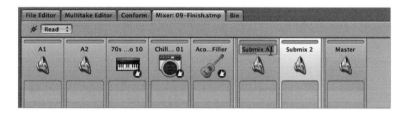

A text field appears.

2   Type *EFX*.

3   Rename Submix 2 *Soundtrack*.

Changing Icons

At the top of each track and submix in the Mixer is an icon. Like a name, an icon provides a quick visual reference indicating the sound that a track or submix contains. Let's change the icons on our submixes now.

1   On the Soundtrack submix, double-click the icon.

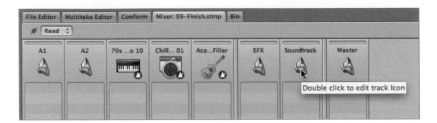

A menu of icons appears.

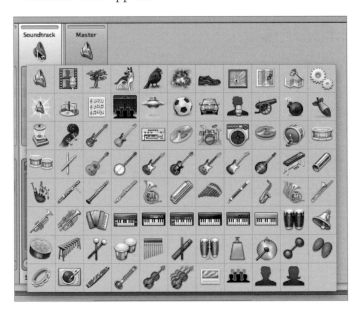

2 Choose the Sheet Music icon to reflect the fact that the Soundtrack submix contains music.

3 Choose an appropriate icon for the EFX submix.

Adding DSP Effects to Mixer Tracks

In previous lessons, you've explored the process for adding effects to individual
clips in a track. That's great if you need to adjust the sound of small parts of a
larger track, but what if you want to apply the same effect to all the clips in a
track at once? Happily, that is easily achieved by applying an effect as an "insert"
on a track or submix.

> **NOTE ▶** The term *insert* comes from the days when audio engineers used
> old-school hardware mixing consoles and hardware effects units. Back
> then (and even today in some studios), audio engineers used patch cords
> to connect effects units to audio channels on mixing consoles. These patch
> cords were literally inserted into receptacles in the mixing consoles, lead-
> ing to the terminology we use today.

In the following steps you will insert a dynamic range compressor into the
EFX submix. The reason is simple: If you look at the waveform of the plane in
track A2, you can see there is a big difference between the loudest portion of
the audio clip (when the plane flies by the camera) and the quietest portion
of the clip (when the plane is off in the distance). This in turns means the

plane is too loud compared to the soundtrack as it flies by the camera, and too quiet compared to the soundtrack at all other times. A dynamic range compressor can be used to even out the volume of the sounds in the track (or in this case, the submix) so they hit your ears at a more uniform volume.

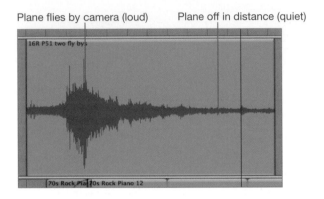

1   Control-click an empty effects slot in the EFX submix channel strip.

    A shortcut menu appears.

2   Choose Add Effect > Dynamics > Compressor.

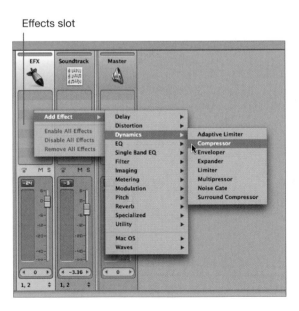

A dynamic range compressor is added to the effects slots of the EFX sub-mix, and the Compressor dialog appears.

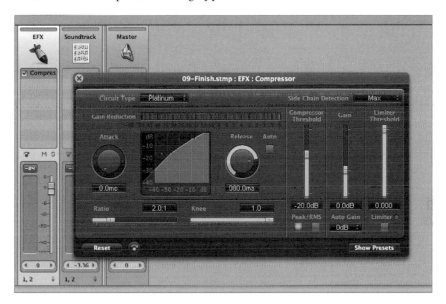

3   In the lower-right corner of the Compressor plug-in dialog, click the Show Presets button.

The Presets drawer slides down from the bottom of the Compressor dialog.

4   Choose the following Compressor preset: User Presets > Compressor
Tools > Hard Squeeze Opto.

> **NOTE ▶** The Hard Squeeze Opto preset is used because it provides dra-
> matic compression so you can clearly hear the results of the preset.

5   In the lower-right corner of the Presets drawer, click the Apply Preset button.

The preset is applied.

6   Play the song from the beginning, and listen to the effect the preset has on the sound of the plane.

> **NOTE ▶** You may need to adjust the volume of the EFX submix to better place the sound of the plane into the mix . . . that choice is now up to you!

7   Press the spacebar to stop playback.

Bypassing Effects in the Mixer

Bypassing effects to hear the original sounds is an old and valuable mixing trick. In fact, it may even be an essential one, because temporarily bypassing effects after they are applied helps you judge the original sound against the sound to which you've applied the effect. You can thus determine if, in fact, the effect is adding to the quality of your mix or subtracting from it. You can bypass effects by using either the bypass button in the effect's dialog, or deselecting the effect in the Mixer. Let's look at both techniques now.

1   Create a cycle region from bar 7 to bar 11.

This region encompasses the loudest part of the plane flyby in track A2.

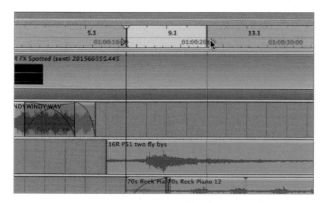

2   Play the cycle region.

3   In the Compressor dialog, click the Effect Bypass button.

The compressor effect is turned off, and you can now hear the uncompressed version of the plane flyby. Let's compare that once more to the compressed version.

4   In the Mixer, select the checkbox beside the compressor effect to unbypass, or turn it back on again.

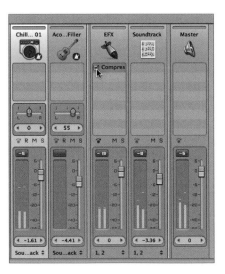

The compressor effect once again alters the sound of the EFX submix.

NOTE ▶ The bypass checkbox on the Mixer offers a handy way to toggle effects when the plug-in dialog is not visible on the screen.

5   Press the spacebar to stop playback.

Exploring Automation

Automation is the real-time keyframing of envelopes in Soundtrack Pro. In previous lessons you explored "static automation"—adding envelope points manually by clicking the envelope lines. While static automation provides a powerful tool for changing sounds over time, it's hard to beat real-time automation. By using real-time automation, you can "play in" envelope changes and make on-the-fly adjustments to the sounds you are hearing as they happen, in much the same way a musician plays an instrument and reacts to the sounds of the surrounding musicians. Real-time automation can provide a much more natural sound to the mix, so it's important to have this arrow in your audio quiver.

Exploring Automation Modes

Real-time automation is accomplished using automation modes. Soundtrack Pro offers three: Latch, Touch, and Read. All three of these modes are accessible from the automation menu in the upper-left corner of the Mixer window, as shown in the figure below.

If you are not familiar with automation modes, a bit of practice will make their use and impact totally clear. To push you in the right direction, these three modes are explained in theory below, and in action in the steps following.

Latch mode is a mode in which Soundtrack Pro "latches on" to the fader position as you control the automation. For example, if you are automating volume and you move the volume fader to 0 dB and then let go, the fader will latch on to the 0 dB setting and remain there until you move it again.

Touch mode is used to temporarily "touch up" your previous automation passes. Essentially, in Touch mode Soundtrack Pro will write automation data whenever you are actually "touching" a slider or fader. But as soon as you let go, the slider or fader returns to the setting that existed *before* you touched up the automation.

Read mode causes Soundtrack Pro to read all previously recorded automation, but does not allow the writing of new automation.

Are the explanations above as clear as mud? If so, don't worry. They will become clearer after you try the Touch and Latch modes and see how they function.

You currently have a cycle region from bar 7 to bar 11. This cycle covers the loud flyby of the plane. In the last section you placed a compressor effect on the EFX submix to level out the sound of this passing plane, but it's still a bit too loud, so let's use automation to "duck," or dip the peak sound of the plane passing by. We'll start with Touch mode, then move on to Latch mode.

1   In the Multitrack Editor, scroll down until the EFX submix is in view.

2   On the EFX submix track, click the disclosure triangle to reveal the envelopes and their automation rows.

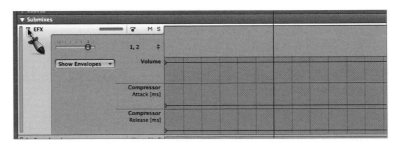

With the envelopes visible, you will see the changes that your automation pass makes to the volume of the EFX submix in the next steps. Additionally, notice there are a couple of new compressor envelopes available. You can use these envelopes to automate settings on the compressor you inserted in the previous section. Compressor, like all other DSP effects, has parameters you can automate as you refine your mixes.

3 In the upper-left corner of the Mixer, set the automation mode pop-up menu to Touch.

4 Position the playhead at the beginning of the cycle region, at bar 7.

5 Press the spacebar to play the cycle region.

6 As the cycle plays, listen to the sound of the plane passing by and drag the EFX submix volume fader down to lower the volume.

7   Once the volume is lowered, release the mouse button.

The volume fader pops back up to its original position.

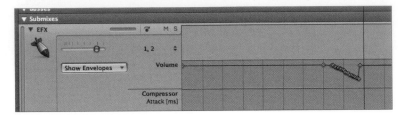

8   Press the spacebar to stop playback.

You are about to set the automation mode to Latch, but you can adjust automation modes only when the song is stopped.

9   Set the automation mode to Latch.

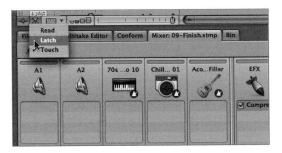

10   Press the spacebar to start playback.

11   As the cycle plays, listen to the sound of the plane passing by and drag the EFX submix volume fader down to lower the volume.

12   Once the volume is lowered, release the mouse button.

The volume latches on to the level where you left the volume fader and does not return to its previous volume level.

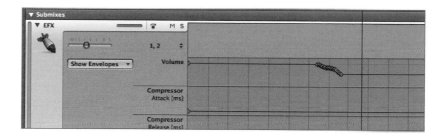

13 Press the spacebar to stop playback.

14 Set the automation mode to Read.

This is an important step, because you don't want to write new automation data every time you move a slider or fader in Soundtrack Pro. If you don't return the automation mode to Read, you'll get a lot of unwanted automation creeping into your song.

Using Buses

Just as the city bus is used for transporting people around your town, so buses in Soundtrack Pro are used to transport sound around the application. Indeed, the submixes you explored earlier in this lesson are a type of bus that allows you to route a group of tracks to certain outputs on your system. Standard buses work in a similar way, except they must send their output to a submix (the way a regular track does), and not directly to an output (as a submix does).

In Soundtrack Pro, buses are mainly used for adding DSP effects to a group of tracks simultaneously. For example, you might have four dialogue replacement tracks recorded by the same actor, and these tracks all need a slight reverb to make the dialogue feel as though it had been recorded in a church cathedral.

As long as the recording environment didn't change between recordings, these tracks will all need to have the exact same reverb, with the exact same settings applied. Instead of applying four different instantiations (copies) of the reverb (one for each track), you can simply instantiate the reverb on a bus, and then send the four tracks to the bus for processing. This not only saves you time while setting up the reverb, but also saves you processor power, because you now have one reverb doing all the work, instead of four separate copies. And of course, if you need to alter the sound of the reverb down the road, you just change it once on the bus, instead of several times on the four separate tracks. There are many benefits of using buses, so let's take a look at how to set them up.

Creating a Bus

In the steps below you'll learn how to add the same reverb effect to multiple tracks by using a bus. Certain effects are more suited to buses than others. For example, dynamic range compressors and equalizers are meant to change the sound of the entire track immediately. They do not persist through time, and in general they work best when inserted on submixes.

Creative effects like reverbs and delays, on the other hand, do persist through time. They continue to make sound even after the original signal has passed, and consequently, they must be mixed back into the original signal. These effects usually have a "dry/wet" setting that lets you mix the effect with the source signal. These effects are ideally suited for use with buses, as you'll learn later in this lesson.

> **NOTE** ▶ If the effect has a dry/wet setting, it is a good effect to use on a system bus.

You can't jump on a bus if there's no bus at your stop. Before using a bus in Soundtrack Pro, you have to create one.

1   From the Multitrack menu, choose Add Bus (Control-Command-T).

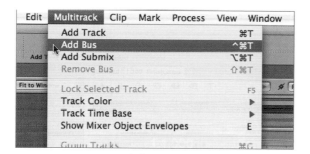

A new bus is added to the Mixer, and it also displays in the top portion of the Tracks tab. In keeping with the left-to-right signal flow we saw earlier in this lesson, the bus is placed between the tracks and the submixes. From this we can deduce that signal passes from tracks, to buses, to submixes, and out via the Master fader on the far right of the Mixer.

Naming Buses

You've heard it a thousand times before, but it's still useful advice: *always use appropriate names.* You'll soon add a reverb to this bus, so let's name it in a representative fashion.

1   In the Mixer, click the name at the top of the bus channel strip.

    A text field appears.

2   Name the bus *My Reverb*.

Using Sends

A send is like a virtual patch cord that connects a track to a bus. Signal is quite literally sent down the send from the track to the bus. To get a feel for this, let's play the song and send the signal from a track to the new bus.

1   Create a cycle region from bar 21 to bar 25.

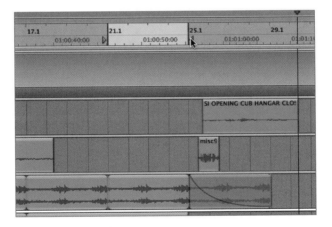

2   Play the cycle region.

As the region loops, you'll be able to hear the effect that adding a send has on the sound of the music in your project.

3   On the Chilled Beats channel strip in the Mixer, Control-click the effects slot area and choose Add Send > To My Reverb.

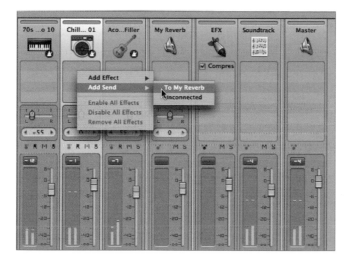

Instantly, your audio grows louder. This is because the Chilled Beats track is now playing through both its own track and the My Reverb bus. In essence, the beats have doubled in volume.

4   Lower the My Reverb volume to approximately *–20*.

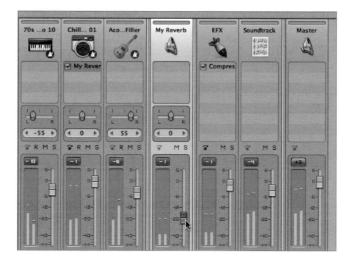

The volume of the beats lowers as you drag down the My Reverb volume fader and pull signal out of the final mix.

5   Double-click the bus volume fader to return it to its default setting of 0 dB.

> **NOTE ▸** Sends can be either pre- or post-fader. To adjust the type of send you're using, select the track and click the Effects tab. Click the disclosure triangle beside Send, and you'll find settings you can use to fine-tune the signal sent through the send to the bus.

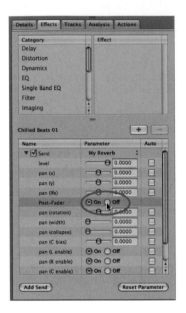

Working with Effects on Buses

In the next steps you'll add reverb to the new bus. For this example, we'll use the Space Designer reverb. This is a good reverb for two reasons: It sounds great, and it's a perfect effect to apply to a bus because it allows you to adjust the amount of source (dry) signal you use, relative to the "effected" (wet) signal. This is vitally important when using effects on a bus because you want to eliminate all source signal passing through the bus so you don't double the signal coming out of the source track. Doing so can cause unexpected volume and phase problems, as you'll see in a moment.

1   On the My Reverb bus channel strip, Control-click the effects slot area and choose Add Effect > Reverb > Space Designer.

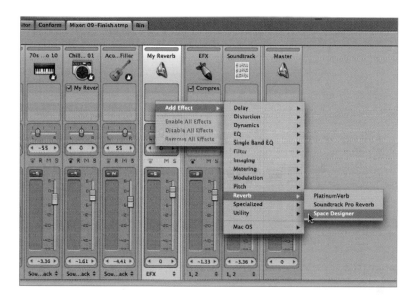

The Space Designer reverb appears and you can instantly hear the effect it has on your cycle.

A bit of reverb sounds great, but the trick is really in how you apply the reverb to your source signal. Look closely at the Space Designer's upper-right area. Notice that there are four sliders, and the ones on the right are called Rev and Dry. These two sliders control the amount of the reverb (the wet signal) and the amount of the source (the dry signal) that are mixed together to produce the final sound.

You already have dry signal coming directly out of the Chilled Beats track, so there's no need to introduce more of that same signal here in the reverb bus. Consequently, you should *remove* any dry signal from this bus.

2   Set the Dry slider to *0* by dragging it to the bottom.

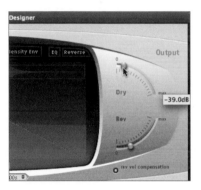

Now, only wet signal is coming out of the My Reverb bus, and that's the way you want it. Mixing like this will help you avoid unexpected volume or phase issues that can occur when two versions of the same sound are played on top of each other, and that's an important step in getting the best possible sound every time you mix.

3   To make the effect more pronounced, drag the Rev slider to the top.

That's a lot of reverb. But don't worry: All you've done so far is increase the volume of the wet signal as opposed to the dry signal coming out of the Chilled Beats track. You can now adjust the volume of the My Reverb bus itself to lower the volume of the reverb relative to the source track.

4   Set the My Reverb bus to a volume of approximately –30 dB.

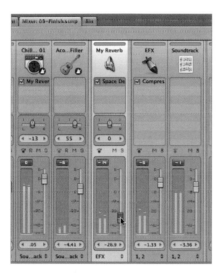

5   Send the Acoustic Guitar Filler track to the My Reverb bus.

Now you have two tracks playing through one reverb. Just imagine the creative possibilities . . . then try some out.

Using the Master Channel

The Master channel is the gatekeeper to your final mix. This channel is like Grand Central Station, collecting all of your tracks in a single destination and sending them happily on their way out of Soundtrack Pro. While you can apply effects such as a limiter or equalizer to the Master channel to tailor the finished sound, the single biggest value of this channel is ensuring that the volume of your finished mix is appropriately set.

There's only one hard rule for volume and the Master channel: Under no circumstances may you ever clip the Master channel by sending out a signal with volume peaking past 0 dB. You can easily see if you've clipped the Master fader by looking at the peak indicator; if you have clipped it, you can then adjust the Master volume fader.

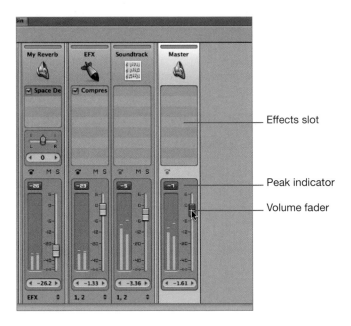

Clipping aside, the output volume you choose depends entirely on the standards set for the format your audio will be delivered in. Here are some common standards:

Media	Peak volume	Average (RMS) volume
CD-Audio	0 dB	–6 dB
Broadcast TV	–6 dB	–12 dB
Theatrical Movie	–6 dB	–31 dB
Webstream	–3 dB	–12 dB
DVD-Video for Theater (AC-3)	–6 dB	–31 dB
DVD-Video for Television (PCM)	–6 dB	–12 dB

The table above refers to both peak and average volume levels. The peak volume level is the loudest level your project reaches. You're accustomed to seeing this level reflected in the peak and hold meters used by Soundtrack Pro. Average volume level takes into account certain other principles to return a weighted average of the volume over time. This gives you a much more accurate representation of the subjective volume of the audio as your ears hear it, and this is the volume level commonly referred to in video terminology. Fortunately, Soundtrack Pro contains a meter that will let you see average as well as peak volume levels. Let's look at it now.

1   On the Master channel strip, Control-click the effects slot area and choose Add Effect > Metering > MultiMeter.

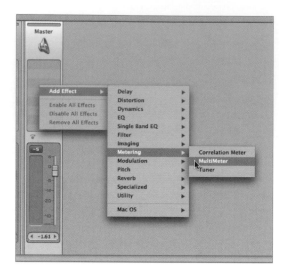

The MultiMeter opens.

2 Press the spacebar to play the song, and watch the MultiMeter.

On the right edge of the MultiMeter there is an output level meter. The bars in this meter display two colors. Light blue is the peak volume for the channel, while dark blue is the average (RMS) volume.

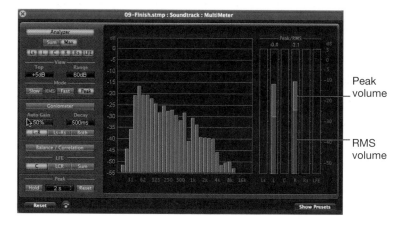

NOTE ▶ You probably noticed that there are six separate channels displayed in the MultiMeter, even though only two channels (stereo) are being used at the moment. This is because under the hood Soundtrack Pro is all surround, all the time. Even when you're mixing in stereo, Soundtrack Pro is still keeping track of all the channels in the surround spectrum, which in turn makes it easy to do both surround and stereo mixes of the same project. Intrigued? Read the appendix on surround mixing to learn more.

3   As you mix, keep an eye on this meter and make sure your output volume levels match the standard for the delivery format for which you are creating your audio.

Lesson Review

1.   Why does a cycle region help when mixing?

2.   What are submixes used for?

3.   What are buses used for?

4.   If you apply a reverb to a bus, what should the "dry" setting be set to?

5.   True or false: If your project contains one or more buses, the signal always travels through the Master channel *before* it is fed to a bus.

Answers

1.   Using a cycle region, you can play a certain section of the song repeatedly, which allows you to become familiar with the sounds it contains as you mix.

2.   Submixes are a collection of similar tracks. You can use a submix to control the volume and pan, or apply effects to several tracks at one time.

3.   Buses let you apply a single instantiation of a DSP effect to multiple tracks at once.

4.   If a reverb is applied to a bus, you should set the "dry" setting to 0.

5.   False. Signal passes from left to right through the Mixer, starting at tracks, then progressing to buses, submixes, and finally the Master channel.

10

Lesson Files   APTS-SoundtrackPro > Lesson 10 > 10 Original Sound
Edit.stmp

APTS-SoundtrackPro > Lesson 10 > 10 Changed Picture
Edit.fcp

Time   This lesson takes approximately 60 minutes to complete.

Goals   Understand the parallel workflows of picture and sound editors

Send revised picture edits to Soundtrack Pro from Final Cut Pro

Conform a sound edit to a revised picture edit

Review and approve clip changes

Learn how to compare projects

Manage the conform process

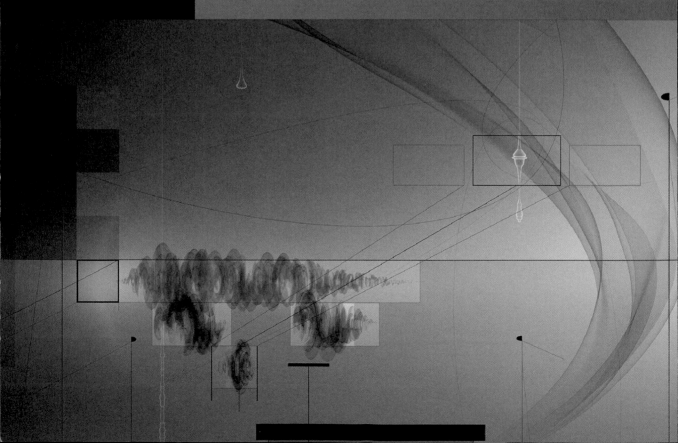

Conforming Multitrack Projects

As any editor will tell you, the editorial process, by definition, involves change. On large productions in which editorial chores are split between "picture editor" and "sound editor," any changes introduced into the process can get time consuming and costly.

Consider this scenario: You are the sound editor on a television show and you're working feverishly to sweeten and mix the show before your looming deadline. You've been told "the picture is locked" (a sometimes-dubious term meaning that no further changes to the picture will be made). Then the phone rings. As is the prerogative of every producer or director, yours tells you that the picture will, in fact, be going back to the editor for changes. Of course, this news comes to you on a Friday afternoon with implications of an entire weekend spent manually changing your sound edit to match the new picture edit, a process known as "conforming."

Fortunately, Soundtrack Pro has a tool, called Conform, that takes the drudgery out of this process. It makes the task much more efficient and less prone to error.

Working in Parallel

One of the benefits of working in Final Cut Studio is that the picture and sound editor can work in parallel, as opposed to working sequentially, as picture and sound editors must do with other software platforms. Assuming the picture was cut in Final Cut Pro and the sound mix performed in Soundtrack Pro, both the sound and the picture editor (sometimes the same person) can work happily and independently in their respective worlds, then later merge their projects into one reconciled Soundtrack Pro multitrack project using the Conform tool.

To see how this process works, open and examine a Soundtrack Pro multitrack project that has been "finished" by the sound editor.

1   If Soundtrack Pro is not open, open it by clicking its icon in the Dock.

2   Choose File > Open and navigate to the Lesson 10 folder.

3   Open the file **10 Original Sound Edit.stmp**.

4   Press Shift-Z to fit the Timeline to the window and press the spacebar to play the scene.

   This is a short scene from the **Blind Date** sequence you worked on in Lesson 3. This multitrack project was originally sent from Final Cut Pro. The sound editor has added a few surround sound effects tracks (in orange) and a music track (in blue).

5   Press the End key to move your playhead to the red marker indicating the end of the Timeline.

   Look at the timecode window and make a mental note that the duration of this scene is 58:00 (58 seconds).

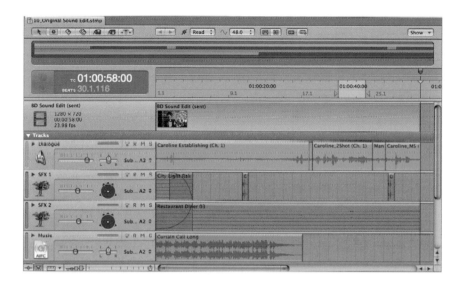

Importing Changes from Final Cut Pro

While all this sound work has been going on in Soundtrack Pro, the picture editor has been making the changes mandated by the producer in Final Cut Pro. You will need to open the revised picture edit to see the changes, then send a new multitrack project based on those changes over to Soundtrack Pro and conform the two projects.

1   If Final Cut Pro is not open, open it by clicking its icon in the Dock.

2   Choose File > Open and navigate to the Lesson 10 folder.

3   Open the file **10 Changed Picture Edit.fcp**.

In the Timeline you should have open two sequences: *BD Original Edit* and *BD Revised Edit*.

4   Click the *BD Original Edit* sequence tab to make it active and play through the scene.

> **NOTE ▸** This is the original edit that was sent to the sound editor for sound finishing. As you can see in the duration column of the Browser, the sequence duration is 58:00, which matches the duration of the multitrack project currently open in Soundtrack Pro.

5   Click the *BD Revised Edit* sequence tab to make it active and play through the scene.

Markers have been placed in the sequence where content has been removed. Seven seconds have been removed from the establishing shot of Caroline walking into the café. Also, at timecode 01:00:43:09, 1 second has been removed from the head of Caroline's reaction shot. If you look back in the Duration column of the Browser, you will see that the new duration for the sequence is 50:00.

Sending the Revised Edit to Soundtrack Pro

The revised picture edit must now be sent to Soundtrack Pro for conforming.

1   In the Browser, Control-click the *BD Revised Edit* sequence, and from the shortcut menu, choose Send To > Soundtrack Pro Multitrack Project.

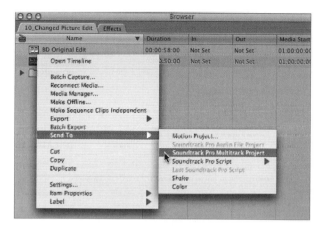

A Save dialog appears.

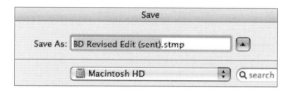

2 Save your sent project file with the default name.

> **NOTE ▶** While you could rename the sent project file, it is better to leave the default name, because it matches the name of the sequence you are sending it from. That will make it easier for all the editors involved to keep track of the picture changes throughout the finishing process.

In the lower section of the dialog are some important options. If you are planning on finishing your audio on another system, you will want to choose Fully Rendered Video. This option will make a self-contained movie of your video that includes all effects, titles, and graphics rendered into it. Instead, for this exercise, we'll leave Base Layer Video selected, which means you will essentially make a reference movie that relies on the original media files on your hard disk and doesn't include any effects. In general, unless you are planning on handing off your work to a sound editor to finish on another system, it's best to leave Base Layer Video selected because of the time and hard disk space it will save you.

The checkbox labeled "Save project with the latest clip metadata (recommended)" is the most important with regard to the conform process. The metadata that is saved along with your movie will give Soundtrack Pro crucial information about what has changed in the multitrack project you are sending. Not selecting this box will compromise Soundtrack Pro's ability to accurately conform your projects.

Conforming Projects

In Soundtrack Pro you should now see two project tabs side by side in the Project pane for Original Sound Edit and BD Revised Edit.

The BD Revised Edit project is dialogue only. As the sound editor, your job is to integrate the changes from this sent Final Cut Pro project with your original sound edit project.

1   In the lower pane, click the Conform tab.

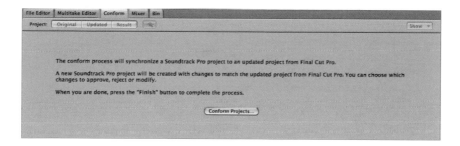

A few lines of text inform you what is about to happen when you click the Conform Projects button. In a nutshell, by clicking the button you will be creating a third project that merges the two projects. You will then be given choices regarding how to reconcile any changes brought about by the conform process.

2   Click the Conform Projects button.

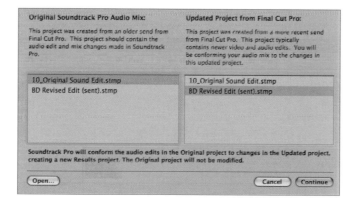

The conform process is initiated and a dialog appears. In the left box, the Original Sound Edit is selected by default. Projects selected in the left box are projects that contain the original audio edit. In the right box, the BD Revised Edit is selected. Projects in the right box are projects that contain the revised, or updated, project that was sent from Final Cut Pro.

3   Click the Continue button.

NOTE ▶ If the first two original projects have not yet been saved, FCP will prompt you to save them first.

In the Project pane, a third, Untitled tab appears next to the other open projects. This project is the "result" project created by the conform process.

If you look in the Conform tab in the lower pane, you will see a large list of clips arranged in a column layout similar to Final Cut Pro's Browser. This area is called the Conform worklist, and it's essentially a sound-change list. That is, it displays all the clips that may have been moved or changed in some way by the conform process.

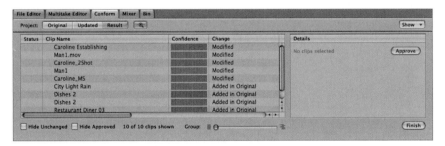

Reviewing Changes

The next step is to go through the worklist to review and verify that every change made to the position and/or duration of your clips is correct. Before doing so, you may find it helpful to maximize the screen real estate for the worklist so you can easily read all the column data.

1   Press Control-D, then press Control-A.

These keyboard shortcuts hide the right and left panes.

2   In the Conform tab, click the button with the magnifying glass icon.

This button is used to identify which clips in the Timeline you are reviewing.

3   Select the topmost clip in the worklist, **Caroline Establishing.**

In the Timeline you will see the clip in dark green, indicating that it is selected.

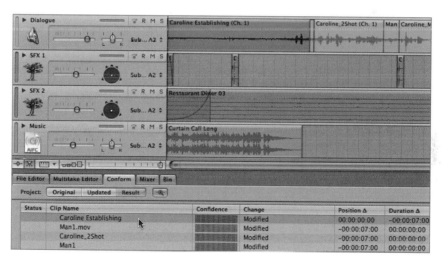

4   Select the **Restaurant Diner 03** clip in the worklist.

The **Restaurant Diner 03** clip appears in dark orange, indicating it is selected. This is a helpful feature for quickly locating and identifying clips in the Timeline that you are reviewing.

NOTE ▸ You can Command-click in the worklist to add to your selection in the Timeline. Additionally, selected clips also appear in yellow in the Global Timeline view.

Viewing Clip Details

To see how a clip was changed, you will need to load the clip into the Details section of the Conform tab.

1   Select the **Caroline Establishing** clip in the worklist.

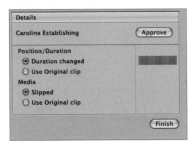

In the Details section, you will see the name of the clip and what specific changes Soundtrack Pro made to the clip.

There are two basic types of changes: Position/Duration changes and Media changes. As you can see from the figure, the duration of this clip was changed, as was the clip's media. To see why Soundtrack Pro made these choices you'll need to look in the worklist.

In the first row in the Position Δ column, you will notice that the value reads 00:00:00:00. This tells you that the clip's original position in the Timeline did not change. However, in the Duration Δ column, you will see a value of –7 seconds. (The delta Δ symbol denotes a change in value.)

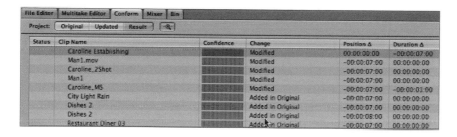

As you may recall, this was the first clip from the revised edit, which had 7 seconds trimmed from the head of the shot. In order for Soundtrack Pro to maintain the clip's original position, the underlying media needed to be slipped 7 seconds.

Approving Changes

Now that you have reviewed and verified the changes that were made to the clip, you are ready to approve the clip. In the Details section is the Approve button. The approval process can be approached in different ways depending on the project's complexity. In one approach, the sound editor simply plays back the conformed Timeline to make sure any audio files have not been altered inappropriately. If audio clips are not in their proper locations relative to the picture, changes can be made directly in the Timeline using Soundtrack Pro's editing tools.

In another approach, the sound editor uses both the worklist and the Timeline to verify the other's accuracy. In this approach, the worklist presents changes to the audio more objectively, giving the editor critical feedback as to how Soundtrack Pro executed a given change. This approach allows the sound editor to make editorial changes directly in the worklist rather than in the Timeline.

In the steps that follow we'll look at the process of approving a clip using the second approach.

1 Click the **Caroline Establishing** clip in the worklist.

By looking at the column data for Duration Δ, you will find that the duration of the clip has changed by 7 seconds.

2 Press Home to move the playhead to the beginning of the Timeline and press the spacebar to play the clip.

Playing the clip in the Timeline is necessary to verify that the conform process made the change correctly. If all looks and sounds as it should, approve the change.

3 Click the Approve button for the **Caroline Establishing** clip.

After approving the clip, a checkmark appears in the Status column and the clip's details are grayed out. Approving a clip is really nothing more than flagging a clip to remind you that it has been reviewed. Once you click Approve, the button changes to an Edit button.

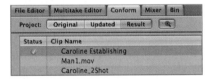

4 To review the clip again, click the Edit button.

So what exactly are you doing when approving a clip using the Approve button? Well, the short answer is, absolutely nothing. When you ultimately click the

Finish button, the changes are executed whether you've approved a change or not. So that raises a second question: Why approve in the first place? The answer is, the approval process is not for Soundtrack Pro's benefit but for your own.

The entire approval process simply entails running through a visual checklist to remind you which clips have been changed correctly during your review and which ones need further review and/or editing. It also saves you from having to review clips more than once.

Comparing Projects

Now let's look at an instance in which Soundtrack Pro made a poor decision in terms of clip position.

1   In the worklist, select the lower **Dishes 2** clip.

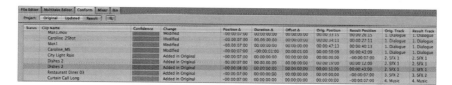

In the Position Δ column, this clip has a delta value of –8 seconds. This simply means that the clip was moved earlier in the Timeline by 8 seconds. If you look in the column Orig. Position, you will see that the clip position before the conform process was at 01:00:51:00. The Result Position column informs you that, afterward, the new position for the clip is 01:00:43:00, exactly 8 seconds earlier.

While all these numbers are helpful in analyzing what has taken place, it is still an academic exercise until you actually check the clip's position in the original project and compare it to the updated project.

2   Press Control-A to reveal the Video tab in the left pane.

Just below the Conform tab you'll see three buttons. These buttons will allow you to toggle between the Original, Updated, and Result projects in the Project pane.

3   Click the Original button.

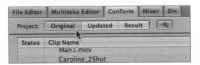

In the Timeline, the original project is displayed.

4   Move the Timeline to just before the **Dishes 2** clip (around 01:00:50:00) and press the spacebar to play it. Keep an eye on the picture as you listen for the dishes sound effect to come in.

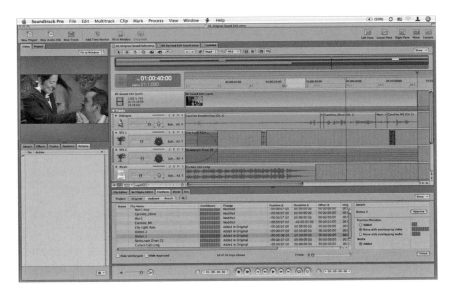

In this project the lead character, Caroline, is playing with the newspaper nervously. We hear the clink of dishes and silverware just before she begins speaking.

You will now compare the Result (conformed) version of the project to see and hear where the dishes sound effect was placed.

5   Click the Result button.

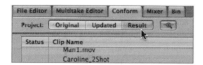

6   Move the playhead to just before the second dishes clip (around 01:00:42:00) and press the spacebar to play it. Keep an eye on the picture as you listen for the dishes sound effect to come in.

This time we hear the dishes while we are still on the shot of the man she is speaking to—which means they've come in a bit too early. We will need to make an adjustment to the clip in the Details section.

Adjusting Clip Placement

To alter the clip's position in the Timeline, you will need to return to the Details section.

1   Make sure the **Dishes 2** clip is still selected in the worklist.

In the Details section there are some options to consider with regard to clip position. Basing its decision on the metadata of the original and revised edits, Soundtrack Pro kept the sound effect aligned with the original video frame it was aligned to, which makes the effect come in too early.

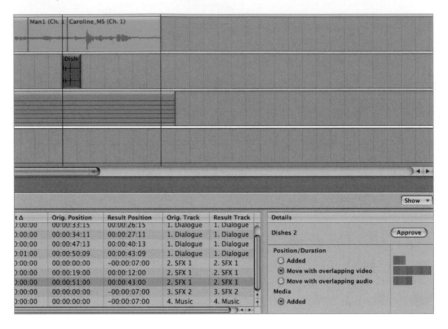

2   In the Position/Duration area of the Details section, select "Move with overlapping audio."

Selecting this option forces the clip to move and align itself with the over-lapping audio. In this case, because the sound effect was initially placed under the **Caroline_MS** audio clip in the original edit, the clip is moved in relation to the original audio with which it was aligned.

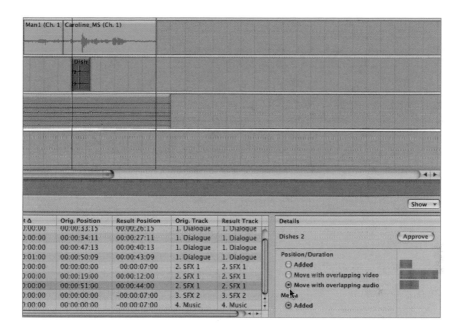

Notice that in the Confidence column, Soundtrack Pro is less certain about this new position. All factors considered, Soundtrack Pro does its best to make an intelligent decision about where to place a clip. At the end of the day, however, you as the sound editor will be the final arbiter of whether the edit works or not. If you need to, you can always move the clip manually.

3 If you are happy with the clip placement, you can click the Approve button and move on to the next clip in the worklist.

NOTE ▶ The approval process is for your tracking and management purposes only. As previously noted, Soundtrack Pro will ultimately create a finished project based on the current clip locations regardless of the clip's approval status.

Filtering, Sorting, and Grouping Clips

Now that you have the basic workflow for reviewing and accepting changes, let's look at some ways you can manage your workflow, particularly with projects that contain hundreds of clips. At the bottom of the Conform tab are some options for hiding and grouping your clips.

Filtering

You can clean up your worklist by clicking one of two filtering checkboxes.

1 Click to select the Hide Approved checkbox.

Selecting this option will remove from view any clips that have check-marks by them. As you approve clips they will automatically disappear from the worklist.

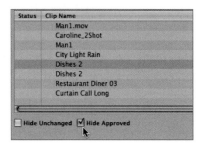

2 Click to select the Hide Unchanged checkbox to remove from view any clips in the Change column that were not modified in any way.

Sorting

As mentioned earlier, the worklist is similar in form and function to Final Cut Pro's Browser.

1 To sort your worklist, click a column header. Here you can sort by criteria such as duration, position, confidence, and so on.

Grouping

You can also create groups of clips to make reviewing and approving easier to manage.

1 Drag the Group slider to the right.

Two separate groups are created.

2 Select either group.

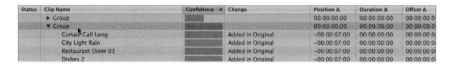

All clips in the Timeline that belong to that group are selected. This makes it easier to approve a batch of clips that you are confident are correct.

3 Click the Approve button, and all clips within the group are flagged in the Status column with a checkmark.

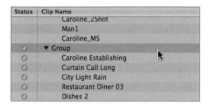

4 Drag the Group slider to the left to return all clips to individual listings.

Finishing

If you are satisfied that all the clips are in their proper places, it's time to click the Finish button to complete your conform and get on with your life.

1 Click the Finish button in the lower right of the Details section.

A dialog will appear asking if you want to finish conforming. You are also heavily warned that there is no going back.

2 Click OK or press Return.

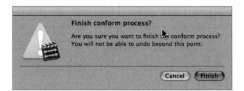

You now have a brand-new Soundtrack Pro project containing your original sound edits reconciled with the changed picture edit. Make sure you save this project, as it is still untitled. If further picture edits are required, you can then conform any new edits with this conformed sequence as the new "original" project.

Lesson Review

1. Why is it important to save project metadata during the conform process?
2. Does the conform process create a new Soundtrack Pro project?
3. What is the Conform worklist?

4. True or false: Only by clicking the Approve button can you instruct Soundtrack Pro to save changes to a project made in the Conform process.

5. Is it possible to approve more than one clip at a time?

Answers

1. The metadata provides Soundtrack Pro with crucial information about what has changed in the multitrack project you are sending.

2. Yes, the sound editor can approve, reject, or modify changes nondestructively and then save the resulting project.

3. The Conform worklist is a sound-change list in which Soundtrack Pro displays all the clips that may have been moved or changed in some way by the conform process.

4. False. When you ultimately click the Finish button, the changes are executed whether you've approved a change or not. The approval process is for tracking and management purposes only.

5. Yes, by using the Group slider to create groups of clips to make reviewing and approving easier to manage. This is helpful in projects where the editor may have hundreds of clips to conform.

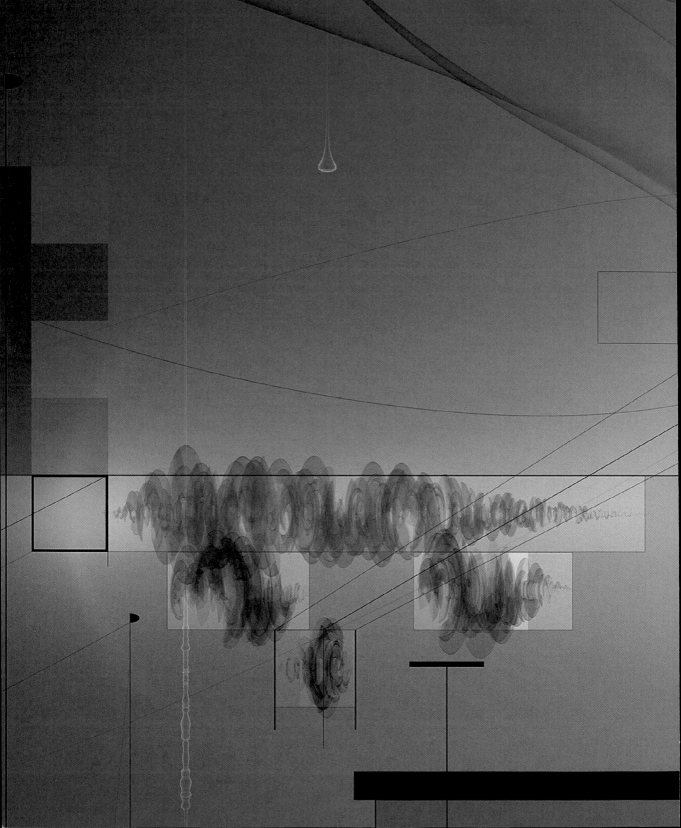

Appendix

Setting Up for Surround Mixing

You may not know it at first glance, but in Soundtrack Pro, you're mixing in surround all the time. Indeed, Soundtrack Pro's architecture was designed from the ground up with surround mixing in mind. Even when you're mixing a stereo soundtrack, you're just using the left and right channels of an otherwise surround signal path. The benefit of this architecture is that you can easily switch from surround to stereo and back again while mixing your projects. And this has definite advantages, because you can create both surround and stereo downmix versions of a project, *in the same project*.

You need to configure two things in Soundtrack Pro to mix in surround: the panner and the submix output. If you don't properly configure both their settings, you'll end up with a stereo mix. With that in mind, let's set up Soundtrack Pro for surround mixing.

> **NOTE ▶** You also need an audio interface with at least six outputs and a surround monitoring system to mix surround. You cannot mix surround using the digital outputs on the back of your computer, because they send only compressed signals, and Soundtrack Pro can't do those kinds of calculations in real time, on the fly.

Setting the Surround Panner

All of Soundtrack Pro's stereo panners hide a deep secret—they are actually surround panners in disguise. More to the point, the stereo panners allow you to access only the left and right channels of the surround signal path at the core of Soundtrack Pro. But you can easily change this.

1   Control-click the panner for any track, and choose Use Surround Panner.

The stereo panner turns into a surround panner.

You are now mixing this track in surround. But the signal going into the submix is still stereo, so you'll need to change that next.

NOTE ▶ You can change the panner on channels in the Mixer in exactly the same way.

Choosing a Surround Submix

With the surround panner turned on for the track, it's time to ensure that your submix is routed to surround outputs.

1   In the Multitrack Editor, scroll down to Submix 1 at the bottom of the track list.

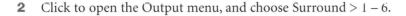

2   Click to open the Output menu, and choose Surround > 1 – 6.

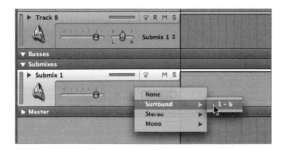

Submix 1 is now routed to surround outputs.

3   Check to ensure that Track 1 is routed to Submix 1.

Using the Surround Panner HUD

The surround panner contains a small white dot called the puck, and dragging the puck around the surround panner moves sounds in the surround audio space. The surround panner is a bit small, making it difficult to precisely position the puck. But Soundtrack Pro also contains a Surround Panner HUD you can use to make precise settings as you pan sounds around the surround field.

1   Double-click the surround panner.

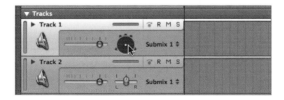

The Surround Panner HUD opens. This HUD contains detailed adjustments you can use to refine your surround mix.

In the center of the Surround Panner HUD is a puck you can drag around to position your sound in the mix. You'll also find sliders to control the rotation, width, and bias of the surround audio space, as well as a slider that lets you adjust how much of the channel's bass frequencies are sent to the low-frequency effects channel. At the bottom of the HUD are level meters for all six channels in the 5.1 spectrum.

Now that you know the lay of the land, you can experiment and have fun with surround mixing.

Index

ONE SIX RIGHT
THE ROMANCE OF FLYING

Footage used in this book is from the feature documentary "One Six Right".
Learn more about this independent film's journey from conception to distribution at:
www.apple.com/pro/profiles/terwilliger

W W W . O N E S I X R I G H T . C O M